The Parent's Complete Guide to YOUNG PEOPLE AND DRUGS

James Kay and Julian Cohen are nationally known figures in drug education. They are health and drug education specialists with an extensive experience of working with young people and parents. James Kay currently manages Healthwise, a health information service in Liverpool, and sits on government advisory bodies on drug abuse; Julian Cohen used to co-ordinate a drugs education project in Greater Manchester and now works with Healthwise and as a freelance trainer and writer. He is the author of many drugs education teaching packs, books and pamphlets for young people, parents and professionals. As well as working all over the UK, James and Julian have lectured about drugs in America, Australia, Canada and in many European countries.

GW00373926

The Parent's Complete Guide to YOUNG PEOPLE AND DRUGS

James Kay and Julian Cohen

VERMILION
London

We would like to dedicate this book to our children
Beth, Lisa, Louisa, Michelle, Robert and Stuart.

1 3 5 7 9 10 8 6 4 2

Copyright © James Kay and Julian Cohen 1998

James Kay and Julian Cohen have asserted their moral right to be identified as the authors of this work in accordance with the Copyright, Design and Patents Act 1988.

First published in the United Kingdom in 1998 by Vermilion
an imprint of
Ebury Press
Random House UK Ltd
Random House
20 Vauxhall Bridge Road
London SW1V 2SA

Random House Australia (Pty) Ltd
20 Alfred Street, Milsons Point, Sydney,
New South Wales 2061, Australia

Random House New Zealand Limited
18 Poland Rd, Glenfield,
Auckland 10, New Zealand

Random House, South Africa (Pty) Limited
Endulini, 5A Jubilee Road
Parktown 2193, South Africa

Random House UK Limited Reg. No. 954009

A CIP catalogue record for this book is available from the British Library.

ISBN 0 09 181553 3

Printed and bound in Great Britain by Mackays of Chatham, plc.

Papers used by Vermilion are natural, recyclable products
made from wood grown in sustainable forests.

Contents

Acknowledgements

We would like to thank the following people who have helped us with the book:

- Helen Galley for her work on the original manuscript.
- The staff and volunteers at Healthwise for their support in all our work with parents and young people.
- The staff from HIT (formerly the Mersey Drug Training and Information Unit) for their helpful comments on a draft of the book.
- The parents we have worked with over the years and, more recently, those who looked at earlier drafts of the book.

Any errors are of course the sole responsibility of the authors.

Introduction

'Drug cocktail kills teenager'
'11-year-old junkies'
'Drugs in city centre club'
'Sharp rise in drug seizures'
'New drug danger warning'

The media headlines about young people's drug use are endless. It can all seem very scary for parents. To make matters worse, lots of youngsters are very casual about it all and just don't understand why their parents get so worried.

This book will help you understand young people's drug use. It is based on the latest information about drugs and the latest research into drug use in the UK. It contains lots of practical advice about what you can actually do as a parent, whether your youngster is using drugs or not.

We want to emphasise at the beginning that there is no need to become over-alarmed about young people's drug use. When you sift the myths from the facts and take a calm look at what young people are up to, it is not all doom and gloom.

Of course there are real dangers from drug use, but it is important to keep them in perspective. We try to take a calm, balanced and practical approach to the subject. We have both worked with parents and youngsters about drug use and are parents ourselves. We share the concerns of parents for their youngsters and we hope that this book reflects the reality of what being a parent is like today.

The book is divided into six main sections:

Part I: This gives information about some of the main questions that parents ask about young people's drug use. We have tried to answer questions honestly and in a practical way.

Part II: This shows what every parent can do, whether their youngster uses drugs or not. It includes activities for both parents and youngsters to work through, as well as information.

Part III: This gives advice on coping in a crisis – when you suspect or know your youngster is actually using drugs or has been arrested, suspended from school, etc.

Part IV: A short conclusion summarising some of the main points in the book.

Appendix I: This is a reference section, which gives more information about the drugs themselves. It includes information on the effects and risks of using different drugs.

Appendix II: This contains information about helping organisations, books, pamphlets, computer programs, Internet sites and other drug education resources to use at home and/or with educational groups.

How to use this book

This book can be used in several ways. You can read it through from cover to cover or just dip into it, picking out the bits you are most interested in. It can be used as a reference book to check out particular pieces of information. You can also turn to it for advice in a crisis.

You can read through the book by yourself but you can also go through all, or some of it, with your partner, a friend or your youngster(s). It contains activities that are designed for you and your youngster working together. We want to encourage you to do this if you can. The book is based on the PACT principle – Parents And Children Talking. We believe that there needs to be much more talking and listening between parents and their youngsters on the drugs issue.

We hope you find it useful.

Last, but not least, we value your views about this book, ways in which it could be improved and any other ideas you have about educating parents about drugs. If you wish to contact us, write to:

Parent's Drug Education
SSU, Healthwise, 1st floor, Cavern Court, 8 Mathew Street,
Liverpool L2 6RE
telephone: 0151 227 4150
e-mail: j.kay@healthwise.org.uk

Part I

QUESTIONS PARENTS ASK ABOUT YOUNG PEOPLE'S DRUG USE

1: How big a problem is it?

It can be very difficult to know how seriously to take the problem of drug use. Stories in the media seem to suggest a tidal wave of drug use sweeping over the country. Everybody seems to be at it. Then it all goes quiet for a while before once again the media are full of it.

How likely is it that your youngster will come across drug use at their school or down your street? What are the chances that they will actually use drugs? If they do use drugs, which drugs are they likely to be? Above all, how dangerous is it really?

There are no quick answers to these questions but recent surveys and research into patterns of drug use amongst young people provide a useful starting-point. Much of the survey information cited below is reported in *Drug Misuse in Britain 1996* published by the Institute for the Study of Drug Dependence. We also report on research conducted in the north-west of England over the last four years.

How many are using what?

The drug most commonly used by young people is caffeine, which is in tea, coffee, many soft drinks and some chocolates.

The second most commonly used drug is alcohol. Surveys show that by the age of 16 well over 95 per cent of youngsters have had an alcoholic drink and that over a third are regular weekly drinkers. Young males are more likely to drink alcohol than females and more likely to drink larger quantities. Recent reports, however, suggest that girls may be catching up as time goes on. Although overall alcohol consumption by young people has not increased in recent years, drunkenness is more common, with young people drinking more alcohol in one session.

Recent years have witnessed the marketing of new drinks of high alcohol content to young people (particularly strong lagers and ciders) and 'alcopops' ('soft' drinks such as lemonade with added alcohol). Much under-age drinking takes place in pubs and as many as two thirds of 16- to 17-year-olds will have had alcohol sold illegally to them. It is often easier for young girls, rather than boys, to drink in pubs and clubs, because they tend to look older.

The third most popular drug of choice amongst young people is tobacco. Just under a third of 16-year-olds smoke on a daily basis and the figures have increased in recent years. Higher proportions of young females smoke than young males. Smoking is also class related. Smoking rates amongst middle-class people are lower than amongst their working-class counterparts. The main target market for the cigarette manufacturers seems to be working-class young women.

It is more difficult to establish the extent of the use of illegal drugs and solvents. This is because young people are often careful to hide their use of drugs. Patterns of illegal drug use amongst young people in different areas tend to vary more between different places and over time than levels of alcohol and cigarette use. However, by putting together information from surveys and research projects that have been carried out in different parts of the UK in the 1990s, a picture can be developed, although it is a complex one.

1. More young people are coming into contact with illegal drugs. A study of 16-year-olds in Greater Manchester and Merseyside found that 76 per cent claimed they had been offered an illegal drug, solvents or poppers (liquid gold or nitrites). A study across England by the Health Education Authority (HEA) found 86 per cent of 20- to 22-year-olds claiming to have been offered illegal drugs.
2. Patterns of drug use are changing across different age groups over time. A major survey in 1994 reported that only 13 per cent of 45- to 59-year-olds said they had taken drugs, whilst 46 per cent of 16- to 19-year-olds claimed to have done so.
3. The age of first use and first contact with illegal drugs seems to be going down.
4. More young people are actually using illegal drugs. In some areas a majority of 16-year-olds report trying an illegal drug (most frequently cannabis) or solvents. The HEA study found 55 per cent of 16- to 19-year-olds and 62 per cent of 20- to 22-year-olds claiming to have used an illegal drug at least once.
5. Whilst the extent of use varies from area to area, what is striking is how widespread the use of drugs now appears to be. Drugs are not only available in inner city areas. Young people and drugs both travel easily. The leafy suburbs and

rural areas have plenty of young people who use drugs, although the much smaller number of young people who use crack cocaine and heroin tend to be concentrated in towns and deprived inner city areas.

6. In the past there have been higher reported rates of illegal drug use amongst males than females. However, some recent surveys have suggested that, at the same age, more young females than males may be experimenting with illegal drugs. This may be because girls 'mature' earlier, mix with boys who are older and so come into contact with drugs at an earlier age than boys. They also are more likely to get into pubs and clubs, where illegal drugs may be sold, at a younger age.

7. Drug use amongst young white people and those of Afro-Caribbean origin is similar. Fewer young people of Asian origin have been reported to use drugs, but informal reports from cities with large Asian communities show they are rapidly catching up their white and Afro-Caribbean counterparts.

8. The most commonly used illegal drug is cannabis. Surveys suggest that there are over 2 million regular users in the UK and over 4 million people may have used the drug at some time. (Many of these people are now parents.) The Greater Manchester and Merseyside survey of 16-year-olds found 45 per cent claiming to have used cannabis at least once and 20–25 per cent being regular users. In some communities use of cannabis is seen as normal and will include use by parents as well as teenagers.

9. The most recent increases in drug use amongst young people have been linked to the popularity of the dance club and rave scene. This has combined particular types of music, dancing and fashion with the use of drugs like ecstasy, amphetamine, LSD and cannabis.

10. Drug use amongst young people tends to increase in the later teen years and early twenties. It then declines through the mid-twenties as people take on more adult responsibilities. Most young people eventually give up illegal drug use whilst continuing with legal substances such as alcohol and tobacco.

Looking at the individual drugs (also see the information about these drugs in Appendix 1), there are some more points that can be made:

Amphetamine

This drug has a long history of use in the UK. There has been a recent revival of interest in its use alongside the dance club scene. Some local surveys show 5–18 per cent of 15- to 16-year-olds claiming to have used it at least once.

Cannabis

See point 8 above.

Cocaine and 'crack' (a form of cocaine)

For information on the differences between crack and powder cocaine, see pages 134–6.

The use of cocaine and crack is not as common as one might think from the media coverage of these drugs. At the beginning of the 1990s a large-scale crack cocaine epidemic was predicted for the UK by some commentators. They claimed it would follow a similar path to that already experienced in some parts of the United States. This has not yet happened in the UK, although both forms of the drug have become more popular amongst some groups. Survey reports still show only very small numbers of the general youth population reporting use of either form of the drug. Local surveys of 16-year-olds have usually found that only about 1 or 2 per cent have used cocaine, but figures may be slightly higher for older teenagers in some areas.

Cocaine powder is still much more expensive than other popular drugs such as cannabis, ecstasy, LSD and amphetamine, although the price has fallen somewhat in the late 1990s. There are increasing informal reports of the use of cocaine powder in clubs, bars and 'café society' in larger cities throughout the UK, but it is still probably outside the price range of most young people who might use some of the other drugs. It is an expensive drug to use in practice not just because of the high unit price but also because of the short duration of the effect. This means that repeated doses would be needed to sustain an evening-long 'high'. Price seems to be the major deterrent to more widespread use although the drug is available in virtually all areas for those prepared to pay for it.

Crack cocaine is also now available in most areas and there are many reports from drug treatment and other local agencies of serious crack cocaine problems in some inner city areas, most notably in London, Manchester and Nottingham. These reports are from deprived areas and use is often chaotic and has been associated with violence and prostitution. It should be re-emphasised that whilst this is a very serious problem for those it directly affects, it still only affects a very small minority of young people.

Ecstasy

This has become a very popular drug on the dance, club and rave scene. It has been estimated that there may be up to 500,000 young people using ecstasy every weekend in clubs. Recent local surveys of 15- to 16-year-olds report 5–14 per cent claiming they had used ecstasy at least once. The English HEA survey in 1995 reported that 15 per cent of 20- to 22-year-olds claimed they had used it. A smaller survey of young people attending some clubs in London and the south-east found that over 80 per cent claimed to have used ecstasy. This is 80 per cent of club-goers, not of the general youth population.

Heroin (and other opioid drugs)

Use of heroin by young people, although increasing, is still relatively rare. In local surveys of 14- to 16-year-olds only about 1 per cent claim to have ever used heroin. The figures may be slightly higher for older teenagers and there has been recent evidence of increased use of heroin and methadone (a drug prescribed by doctors to heroin users) by young people.

Reports to doctors and drug agencies of those having serious problems with these drugs have been increasing each year for over 15 years. In the late 1990s the rate of increase year-on-year has stepped up to over 20 per cent. It is now estimated that there are well over 100,000 serious problem users of heroin and other opioids in the UK. Prices have remained stable over a long period. In real terms, after allowing for inflation, heroin has thus become much cheaper and is now available in virtually every town and city in the UK.

LSD

This was a popular 'hippie' drug in the 1960s. It went out of fashion, but from the late 1980s onwards has again become popular. In local surveys up to 24 per cent of 16-year-olds claim to have used it at least once, but it is only rarely used on a regular basis.

'Magic mushrooms'

These are particularly popular in late summer and early autumn when they grow wild in many areas. Surveys have found that 5 to 15 per cent of 15- to 16-year-olds claim to have used them at least once, but they are only rarely used on a regular basis.

Poppers (nitrites, liquid gold)

These are available from sex and joke shops, clubs and some tobacconists and young people's clothes and record shops. Most types are not illegal to use or to sell. In the past they were popular mainly amongst some gay men but now their use by young people in general is more common. One survey put the number of 16-year-olds claiming to have used them at least once at 23 per cent.

Solvents

This is the inhaling or sniffing of glues, butane gas, aerosols, etc. Use tends to vary greatly from area to area and from time to time. There has been a switch away from the use of glue to the more dangerous use of gas and aerosols. Local surveys show up to 20 per cent of 15- to 16-year-olds claiming to have used solvents at least once. Solvent use tends to go in waves and be the bottom rung of the drugs market. Very few young people use solvents on a regular basis.

Steroids

These are used medically for a number of complaints but there has now been an increase in their non-medical use. They are used by sportspeople and body-builders and increasingly by young people who want a 'beautiful' body. This may include the 'health and fitness' types of youngsters who are not normally associated with drug use. There is not much survey data on the use of steroids, but there are many reports from needle exchange agencies (see page 61) of steroid injectors turning up in substantial numbers to use these services, which were first set up for those injecting drugs such as heroin.

Tranquillisers

Nearly 15 per cent of British adults take these drugs on prescription at some time in each year. Young people, especially girls, are sometimes prescribed them for anxiety or sleep problems. There is also a street trade in tranquillisers. Some young people use them, sometimes combined with alcohol, for their drug effect. It is not known how widespread this is, although some local studies have found up to 10 per cent of 16-year-olds claiming to have used tranquillisers at least once. Also some injectors of opioid-type drugs, such as heroin, use tranquillisers (especially Temazepam) if they cannot get the opioid. This is rare amongst younger age groups.

Finding out more about drug use in your area

Drug use patterns vary widely from area to area and over time. If you want more information about drug use in your locality there are a few places you can go to get this information.

A good place to start is your local library. The larger central libraries will have the most information, but even branch libraries should have some leaflets and contact information. They may be able to tell you about local drug agencies and projects and may have copies of any local surveys into drug use which have been published. They might also have a local press cuttings file.

You can also ring the National Drugs Helpline on 0800 77 66 00. They keep records of drug agencies in many areas and should be able to give you details of projects in your locality. Most specialist drug agencies are happy to talk to the 'worried well' and will have a pretty clear idea about what proportions of local youth are using which drugs. However, it is worth remembering that specialist agencies often deal with very heavy users of drugs like heroin. They may not be as knowledgeable about younger and 'recreational' users of drugs such as ecstasy, LSD, cannabis, etc.

Your local education authority (LEA) should have specialist health education advisers and youth workers who will have done a lot of work on drug issues. You can contact them through the LEA at the local town hall.

A final suggestion is to ask other parents and any local young people you know (and most of all your own youngsters) about what they know about drug use locally. Also look at page 98, 'Know where and how to get help in your area' and Appendix II, 'Where to find out more', page 154.

But is it a problem?

Drug use is now widespread among young people. There are large numbers of teenagers and young adults using a wide range of drugs. There are very few teenagers in Britain today who do not at least know a friend or schoolmate who has used illegal drugs. Even those who choose not to use illegal drugs will probably come across drug use by friends at some time.

How worried should we be about this situation? How dangerous is it really? It should be emphasised that in the large majority of cases, use of drugs by young people does not lead to serious problems. To get matters in perspective, it can help to understand that many young people will only use drugs once or twice or for a short period, and then decide to stop. Others will use more regularly but take care about what they do, much as many responsible adults use alcohol. There are young people who get into health, social, financial or legal problems with drug use, but these are a small minority.

For more information about the different ways young people use drugs, see 'Why do young people use drugs?' page 21. 'What effects do drugs have and what are the dangers?', page 34, describes some of the general risks of drug use, and Appendix I, 'Facts about drugs', page 127, outlines some of the specific risks associated with use of individual drugs.

Drug use is certainly risky and certain drugs and certain ways of taking them are more risky than others. About 1,000 people die each year in the UK as a result of using illegal drugs. In the 1990s between 60 to 150 young people a year have died as a result of volatile substance use (gas or solvent 'sniffing'). Every one of these deaths is a tragedy, but these numbers should be set alongside the 110,000 people a year who die in the UK from the effects of smoking cigarettes. That is about 300 deaths a day. There are also another 20,000 to 30,000 deaths a year associated with alcohol use. Whilst only a few of these tobacco-related deaths will directly involve young people, a significant number of alcohol-related deaths do.

Of course, parents are usually very unhappy to see their son or daughter taking illegal drugs and there has rightly been much concern about recent increases in drug use by young people. The good news for us, as parents, is that only in a small minority of cases does it lead to serious harm. One task we set ourselves in writing this book is to help you to reduce this number still further.

2: Why do young people use drugs?

Young people use drugs in different ways. Some use drugs only for a short time, possibly only once or twice. These are the 'experimenters'. Some go on from experimenting to use the drug in a regular but fairly controlled way, taking care what they use, how much and how often. These are the 'recreational' users. It is described as recreational because the drug use is often used alongside recreational social activities such as going out, dancing, watching films or videos, listening to music and being involved in 'courting' or sexual activity. Most adults are 'recreational' alcohol users. Many young people use illegal drugs in a similar way.

A small group of young people using drugs will come to rely on the feelings that their drug use gives them to help them through their day. They will not be able to carry on functioning without their drugs for long. These we call 'dependent drug users'.

These are important distinctions to make when trying to understand why young people are using drugs. Why a young person experiments with drugs will be very different from why they may go on to use in a recreational or even in a dependent way.

Experimentation

Here are some of the reasons why young people might experiment with drugs.

- Drugs are available. They are there to use, so why not have a go?
- Out of boredom. Nothing better to do – why not have a go when it might be fun?
- Out of curiosity. It sounds interesting, so why not see what it makes you feel like?
- The influence of other people. Some of your friends are doing it and seem to be having a good time. You don't want to miss out or be the odd one out. It's good to be 'one of the crowd' or part of the 'in set'.

- As a protest. You know you shouldn't, but it's fun to rebel sometimes, especially doing things your parents would not approve of – naughty but nice.
- It can be fun and pleasurable changing the way you feel about yourself, other people and the world around you.

None of these reasons reveal any great social or psychological problem in the young drug experimenter. They are the sort of everyday reasons why young people take risks with other things they should not do or which put them in danger – things like stealing from shops, riding motorbikes, using skateboards, joining gangs and playing chicken with traffic. Some of these things are dangerous, illegal and/or downright stupid. But other risky activities are encouraged by most adults as healthy sport. Young people die each year and thousands are injured in sports like football, rugby, climbing, swimming, cycling, canoeing, abseiling, etc. Taking risks, experimenting with new situations and changing the way you feel are normal parts of growing up. Most of the time young people get away with it.

Recreation

Those who go on from experimenting to regular use in a recreational way are getting something else out of their drug use. The reasons why they started using are listed above. They carry on using because they get something they particularly value out of the drug use.

We are so used to talking about the problems of drugs that it can seem strange to talk about the pleasures or benefits. Yet this is what we have to do, if we want to understand why young people use drugs regularly in a recreational way. Reasons may include:

- It is enjoyable. Using drugs can make you feel happy, relaxed, and sexy and, depending on the drug used, full of energy.
- Some drug use fits in well with other social activities and fashions that young people like, such as dancing or listening to music. The drug effect can enhance the pleasure.
- Drugs like ecstasy, LSD and cannabis do not have the nasty hangover effects you get from large amounts of alcohol. They can seem a much nicer 'buzz' and do not result in the same levels of violence as alcohol, according to many young people.

- Drug use may help people feel more confident and communicate more easily. It may also lower inhibitions in sexual situations.
- These days many drugs are cheaper – or at least as cheap – as alcohol.

This begins to sound like an advert for drugs. If it's that good, shouldn't we keep quiet about it or we will have even more youngsters using? This is a key issue for parents. In moderation, and for most young people, drug use is fun and pleasurable and does not lead to many problems. That is why we have hundreds of thousands using ecstasy every weekend and over 2 million or more smoking cannabis each year.

We do no one any favours by avoiding the truth or doctoring it in some way to make it seem worse. We have a big gap in understanding between adults and young people when it comes to drugs. Most of that gap is caused by our reluctance to recognise that, from the young person's point of view, these can be very attractive substances, whether we like it or not. This is not to say that drug use is acceptable, but to face up to the truth that using them can be fun and pleasurable.

Dependency

A small minority of those who use drugs will become dependent on the drug experience as a way of getting through life. (We have given a definition of dependency on page 28.) These are the people who are often called 'addicts'. They tend to be dependent on the heavy sedative drugs like alcohol and heroin and/ or tranquillisers, although dependency on other drug types is possible.

Many people who are dependent on drugs will use them every day. The reasons why some people become dependent on drugs are very different from the reasons for experimentation or recreational use. The reasons for dependency can include:

- The drug use blocks out physical pain. Some dependent users started using in hospital, after operations, but this is rare among younger people.
- The drug use can block out psychological pain. Many people have become dependent on tranquillisers after being prescribed them to cope with the death of a loved one. Others may use

alcohol or heroin every day to block out negative emotions and feelings about themselves, their situation or past experiences. Cocaine, crack and heroin dependency is common amongst some prostitutes. Drug use may 'cocoon' people from what they experience as a very unpleasant world.

- Life can seem dull and empty, particularly if you are poor, unemployed and maybe living in bad housing. What is the point of it? Everyday drug use can float you away and help you to forget your day-to-day worries.
- The daily hustle to make money, score drugs, avoid the police and be part of a drug scene with other people can provide some structure and apparent meaning to an otherwise empty life.

As you can see, these reasons are all much more to do with the physical, social and emotional needs of young people. This sort of drug use is a retreat into the safety and predictability of the drug use experience. This is quite unlike the reaching out into a new and exciting lifestyle that experimenters or recreational users are looking for.

In summary

What can we make of all of this? An early step, when you are looking at what might be drug use in a young person, is to try and work out what is going on for them. What sort of drug use is it? Remember that drug use is a very individual thing and varies depending on the person and their situation. Take care not to jump to conclusions or make assumptions about young people in general and your youngsters in particular. Talk to them, listen to them and get to understand their concerns (you'll find ideas on how to do this in Part II).

Many parents blame themselves or other people if their youngsters use drugs. Remember that drug use is very common amongst young people and can seem a 'normal thing' from their point of view. In many areas a majority of young people have experimented with illegal drugs, but few become dependent. Most young people use drugs because they want to and out of their own choice, without being forced to do so.

3: Where do young people get drugs from?

The drug pusher myth

There is a popular image of the evil drug dealer plying unsuspecting and innocent young people with dangerous drugs. In its most scary form this image has the drug dealer in an ice-cream van outside the school gates dispensing heroin over the counter.

Thankfully this almost never happens. Offering drugs to new 'customers' is a risky business. They might tell someone and the maximum sentence for supplying illegal drugs is life imprisonment. Imagine the treatment a drug dealer would receive from the judge if the offence involved selling direct to youngsters in such a way. Worse still for them, imagine if local parents got hold of them! Even drug dealers have more sense than to run such risks for the chance of making a small amount of new business.

Another myth about the supply of drugs is that dealers will somehow spike the drinks, ice cream or sweets of young people in order to get them hooked on the drugs. The idea is that they will then go on to charge higher prices to make up for the earlier losses. Again this is very unlikely once you think about how this actually might take place. It assumes that:

- dealers have spare supplies for such speculations;
- the spiked young people would know what was making them feel strange;
- they wouldn't tell anyone else about it;
- they would come back to the dealer, money in hand, anxious to repeat the experience.

Your mate – the dealer

Young people usually get drugs in small quantities from friends, older brothers and sisters, other relations or acquaintances. This was confirmed in research in Liverpool where we found that over 50 per cent of young people questioned told us that they got illegal drugs 'from a mate'. Less than 10 per cent used a dealer.

This is because in most cases drugs are not 'pushed' at all but 'pulled'. One person gets hold of some drugs and other young people scrounge some off them, ask them for them or are thankful to be offered some. Somebody in almost every secondary school, youth club or group of young people will know someone who knows someone who can get drugs in this way. Another way it happens is for a group of young people to pool their money and one of them, who knows someone who has some drugs, buys for the group. In addition young people may approach, or be approached by, small-scale dealers in clubs or pubs.

Of course there are larger-scale drug dealers, but most tend to avoid younger people. Youngsters, with their limited incomes and tendency to tell tales, tend to be poor customers. If young people do come into direct contact with 'dealers' these are likely to be small-scale local dealers who are possibly users themselves.

There used to be a clearer distinction between suppliers of drugs like cannabis and LSD and those who sold heroin. With the increase in the variety of drugs these days this distinction may not always hold good. Some people argue that cannabis should be legally supplied so that young people could get hold of it easily without having to make contact with people who might supply them with more dangerous drugs like heroin. Whatever the merits of this case, it seems unlikely to happen in the foreseeable future.

How much does it cost?

The answer is not nearly as much as many parents think. If young people are looking for a good night out with their mates they can get it as cheaply, or more cheaply, using illegal drugs than they can with alcohol.

- In 1998 in London, Liverpool or Manchester £10 spent on cannabis could buy enough to make four or five joints (cannabis cigarettes). This is enough for a small group of three or four young people to get a 'high' for several hours.
- About the same money or very little more will buy a tablet of ecstasy or a 'bag' of amphetamine or heroin.
- At about £2.50 a time, LSD is the cheapest high on the illegal market. One dose can give up to eight hours 'tripping'.
- A bottle of nitrite (poppers or liquid gold) will cost £3–£5.
- Magic mushrooms and solvents may be available free or at very low cost.

Illegal drugs have become much cheaper over the last 10 years in real terms when compared to the cost of alcohol. Given these prices, it is not so surprising that more and more young people are using illegal drugs.

4: What does all this drug language mean?

The language of drugs can seem strange and difficult to understand for many parents. On the one hand there is the obscure technical jargon of the medical profession and those who work with drug users and on the other hand there is the strange street jargon of the drug 'scene' that so many young people use.

Medical/drug professionals' terms

We have given below a short glossary of terms that doctors and drug specialists might use and terms that are in wide popular use. You might want to start by thinking about what you understand by the following terms:

addiction	overdose
dependency	problem drug taker
depressant	psychoactive
drug	psychotropic
drug abuse	sedative
drug misuse	soft drugs
hallucinogenic	stimulant
hard drug	tolerance
hypnotic	withdrawal symptoms
narcotic	

We define these terms as follows:

addiction

This term is usually applied to drugs but can be used with lots of activities that can become compulsive habits, like gambling or playing arcade games. The term 'workaholic' has been used to

describe people addicted to work. With drugs, an addict is someone who uses on an everyday basis and finds it difficult to stop
using. The term is not used so often now by professionals because
it has come to mean so many things to different people. It can also
conjure up misleading stereotypes of drug users. Many prefer the
more precise term 'dependency' (see below).

dependency

Drug dependency is usually divided into physical and psychological.

Physical dependency is when someone has taken drugs in quantity for a time and comes to rely on the use of a drug in order to
feel well and for their body to function 'normally'. It happens
when the body has built up a tolerance (see page 30) to the drug
and in its absence physical withdrawal symptoms (see page 31)
appear. It can only happen with certain drugs, especially depressant drugs like alcohol, heroin or tranquillisers.

Psychological dependency is when the user experiences an overwhelming desire to continue with the drug experience. This can be
because of the pleasurable effects, but is more likely be some sort
of psychological crutch. The drug experience has become a way of
blocking out reality, of making life bearable, of facing the world.
Without the crutch life seems worthless. This can happen with
any drug.

depressant

This describes a drug that depresses or slows down the operation
of the central nervous system. Alcohol, heroin and tranquillisers
are depressants.

drug

There are many different definitions of drug; here we use the term
for any substance which, when taken into the body, changes the
way you think or feel. Our favourite definition is 'drugs are something other people do', reflecting the way we all shy away from
thinking of the substances we use ourselves as 'drugs' and the
way we do not like seeing ourselves as 'drug users'.

drug abuse

Drug abuse is a term very widely used but rarely defined. It
seems to be used most often to describe drug use that is not liked
by society or by individuals. The problem is that societies and

individuals change their minds from time to time about what sorts of drug use is OK. We try to avoid using this term because one person's use seems to be another person's abuse.

drug misuse

This term is very much like drug abuse above and with all its shortcomings. It is sometimes used to mean the illegal use of drugs.

hallucinogenic

This describes a drug that alters perception: the way you see, hear, feel, smell or touch the world. This can mean that these senses can get all mixed up or changed. You may see colours much more brightly perhaps or hear sounds differently. LSD and so-called magic mushrooms are hallucinogenic drugs; the term is also sometimes used to describe ecstasy.

hard drugs

This term has been used to describe what are believed to be the most dangerous drugs such as heroin and cocaine. It is not a term most drug specialists would use because it is too vague. For example is amphetamine a hard drug or not? Is alcohol? Some would say yes, others no, still others would say it depends on how it is taken, how much is taken, etc.

hypnotic

This term is used to describe drugs that help you to sleep – sometimes whether you want to or not! An example is tranquillisers, although other depressant drugs like alcohol and heroin can also have this effect.

narcotic

This comes from a Greek word meaning 'to numb'. It is a bit of an old-fashioned word now but has been used in two ways. Firstly it has been used to describe drugs that have a hypnotic effect – i.e. those that can make you go to sleep. Secondly and in a more general way this term has been used to describe so-called 'hard drugs' like heroin and cocaine.

overdose

This means, as it sounds, taking more of the drug than is necessary to get an effect. It is an over dose. In some cases it can be harmful or even fatal, particularly with sedative drugs like heroin or alcohol.

problem drug taker

Drug specialists use this term to describe anyone who has a problem with their use of drugs. The problems could be legal, physical, psychological or social.

psychoactive

This refers to drugs that are active in the psyche or mind – in other words, the type of drugs we discuss in this book.

psychotropic

This means the same as psychoactive. It is a good example of medical jargon – two obscure words for the same thing.

sedative

This is similar to depressant. It refers to drugs that sedate or depress the central nervous system. They slow things down. Heroin, alcohol, tranquillisers – these are all sedative drugs.

soft drugs

A term sometimes used to describe drugs like cannabis that cannot produce physical dependency. It is contrasted with 'hard drugs' which are generally believed to be much more dangerous. Like the term 'hard drugs', it is a bit vague because people can still have problems using so-called 'soft drugs'. Many drug specialists will not use the term for that reason.

stimulant

This describes drugs that tend to stimulate or speed up the action of the central nervous system. They are almost the opposite of sedative or depressant drugs. Amphetamines (sometimes called speed or whizz), cocaine, caffeine and ecstasy are all stimulant drugs.

tolerance

This is the process by which the body can adapt to the presence of a drug such that you need to take more to get the same effect. The body learns to tolerate the drug in the system. Alcohol, barbiturates, cocaine, crack (a form of cocaine), heroin and amphetamine are all drugs to which the body can build up tolerance.

withdrawal symptoms

These are usually described as a series of symptoms (a syndrome) which can be caused by stopping the use of a drug to which the body has become tolerant. As the body learns to adapt to the drug, it becomes reliant on the drug just to feel normal. Take the drug away and you feel terrible – until the body readjusts back to its normal drug-free functioning. Withdrawal symptoms usually take the form of shivering, shaking, aching joints, running nose, nausea and vomiting – like having flu badly.

What about street language?

Like many other social activities, drug use has its own jargon. Special words have been developed by drug users to describe the drugs, methods of use and other activities involving drug use. This street slang can be fairly obscure as in 'dropping love doves' (taking ecstasy tablets) or 'cranking smack' (injecting heroin). We have included some of the slang words for different drugs in Appendix I, 'Facts about drugs', page 127, to help you understand what is being talked about. But there are some pitfalls to avoid.

Street slang changes – sometimes rapidly. This is partly because it changes when the terms become more widely known. Just when parents and teachers think they have learnt the latest terms they find they are out-of-date. After all, one purpose of street language is to communicate without people like parents and teachers knowing what is going on. Although some terms live for decades, there are others that survive for only a few weeks.

Also, some slang terms mean different things in different places. 'Dope', for example, can mean cannabis or sometimes heroin. In some places it means all illegal drugs. 'Give me the dope' could therefore have at least three potential meanings.

Young drug users themselves are sometimes confused about slang and make mistakes. This is because they want to be seen by their friends as being 'in the know'. We recently came across a young person using the term 'trips' to mean LSD, ecstasy or amphetamine. By the way they used the term it was apparent that they did not know they were describing three different drugs or that 'trips' is most often used to describe the experience of taking LSD. We have also found young people using 'draw' without realising that they were using cannabis or that it was an offence to be in possession of it.

We suggest that you take care using street language. Nothing can be worse than using last year's slang in the mistaken belief that it makes you sound 'hip'. Here are a few guidelines:

- Wherever possible, use the proper name for the drug rather than the slang word, i.e. heroin not smack – unless you are very comfortable with the slang.
- If a young person uses a slang term, check that you have understood it properly: 'Do you mean amphetamine?' 'Do you mean injecting?' and so on. Most young people will be more than happy to explain it to you. They can be like most hobbyists explaining their interest to someone new.
- As always, the key is *communication*. Listen to your youngster. Ask them questions. Acknowledge that they may know more than you do and they will be more likely to open up. Trying to be too clever with your use of slang can get in the way of good communication if you are not careful.

5: What are the different ways of taking drugs?

Mood-altering drugs work by changing the way the brain operates. To do this they need to get into the bloodstream. There are several ways of doing this. Once in the bloodstream the drugs circulate to the brain and the rest of the central nervous system where they begin to have an effect. These effects will usually be depressant or sedative (slowing down), stimulant (speeding up) or hallucinogenic (changing perception). The methods of taking drugs are as follows:

Eating/drinking

Here the drug gets into the bloodstream through the wall of the stomach and the small intestine. The blood containing the drug then has to go through the liver and heart before returning to the heart to be pumped to the brain and central nervous system.

Examples of taking drugs in this way are drinking alcohol, taking tranquillisers, ecstasy or LSD and eating magic mushrooms. When drugs are eaten or drunk the effects come on relatively slowly, usually in 10 to 30 minutes.

Smoking/inhaling vapours

This involves breathing in the smoke and fumes produced by burning drugs or the vapours given off by glues, aerosols and other solvents. Smoke or fumes can be breathed in through the mouth and/or the nose. They then pass into the lungs, on into the bloodstream and then straight to the heart and are then pumped to the brain.

Smoking can be done in a cigarette form (called a 'joint' when it contains cannabis) or by burning the drug directly and breathing in the fumes. With heroin this is sometimes called 'chasing the dragon'. Here the heroin is burnt with a match or cigarette lighter through silver foil. The drug turns into a sticky liquid, which rolls around the foil and has to be chased by the smoker to keep it burning. The fumes are inhaled.

Glues, aerosols and other solvents and nitrites (poppers) all give off vapours which contain mood-altering drugs. They can be put into bags or poured on to rags and the fumes inhaled. Gases, such as butane from cigarette lighter refills are sometimes squirted directly into the mouth. This is particularly dangerous.

Examples of taking drugs by smoking or inhaling include smoking tobacco, cannabis, heroin or crack cocaine, 'sniffing' glues, gases such as butane and other solvents and inhaling nitrites. When drugs are smoked or inhaled the effects tend to come on quite quickly – usually within a minute or so but sometimes in seconds.

Snorting drugs

Some drugs are snorted up the nose in powder form. The drug is then taken into the bloodstream through the membranes in the nose.

Sometimes quite elaborate methods are used to prepare drugs for snorting. Cocaine can be chopped up into a fine powder with a razor blade. This is usually done on a small mirror to make sure that none of it is lost. (Cocaine is very expensive.) Finally the powder is then snorted up through a straw or sometimes a rolled-up banknote.

Examples of drugs which are often snorted are snuff (a form of tobacco), cocaine and amphetamine. Most drugs are not taken in this way.

When drugs are snorted the effects come on within a minute or so, similar to when drugs are smoked or inhaled.

Injecting drugs

Here a solution of the drug is made up which is then injected using a syringe. Injection can be direct into a vein, into fatty tissue or muscles or sometimes just under the skin. Going straight to the vein causes the fastest and most intense 'hit' of all forms of drug use. Usually the effects are felt within seconds.

Drugs which are often injected are heroin (and other opioid drugs), amphetamine, some tranquillisers, steroids and occasionally cocaine.

Injecting is particularly dangerous because of the danger of taking too much in one go (and possibly overdosing) and because of the risk of infection by blood-borne diseases, particularly hepatitis or HIV (the virus that leads to AIDS), if injecting equipment is shared.

For more information about the dangers associated with the different ways of taking drugs see the following section.

6: What effects do drugs have and what are the dangers?

Some people think everyone who takes drugs will end up dead. Some young people seem to think that drug use is one big laugh and not at all dangerous. The truth is somewhere in between. Drug use can never be 100 per cent safe, but is not always as dangerous as many people think.

In order to learn about how drugs affect people and make a careful judgement about the real dangers, it helps to know about the interactions between the drug, the person and the environment. The basic principle is that drug effects are the result of interactions between these three factors. Drug effects are not just produced by the drugs themselves.

The drug aspect is everything connected with the drug itself and how it is used. The person is everything connected with the person who is using the drug. The environment is about what the person is doing at the time and where they are.

The drug

Drugs are not all the same. There are three main categories: sedative, stimulant and hallucinogenic. The drugs, which have a sedative effect (such as alcohol, heroin and tranquillisers), slow down the way the body and brain function. They can have a numbing effect that produces drowsiness if a lot is taken. Other drugs (such as amphetamine, caffeine, cocaine and crack, ecstasy and nicotine) have a stimulant effect, giving a rush of energy and making the user more alert. A third group of drugs (such as LSD and magic mushrooms and, to a lesser extent, cannabis and ecstasy) have an hallucinogenic effect. This means they tend to alter the way the user feels, sees, hears, tastes or smells. (We describe the effects and risks of different drugs in detail in Appendix I, 'Facts about drugs', page 127.)

Some drugs are also potentially more dangerous than others. For example, with sedative drugs like alcohol and heroin there is the possibility of taking a fatal overdose. Such drugs can also badly affect co-ordination, making accidents much more likely. Regularly taking sedatives can also lead to physical dependence and withdrawal symptoms, whilst taking other drugs like cannabis cannot.

Stimulant drugs can produce anxiety or panic attacks, particularly if taken in large quantities. They can also be particularly dangerous for people who have heart or blood pressure problems.

Hallucinogenic drugs sometimes produce very disturbing experiences and may lead to erratic or dangerous behaviour by the user, especially if they are already unstable.

And, of course, some drugs are legal to use and others are not. This means that being involved with certain drugs can lead to a criminal record, a fine and maybe even prison. (See 'What does the law say?', page 42.)

The effects and dangers of drug use will also depend on the following factors.

How much is taken

The more taken the greater the effect and the greater the danger. Taking too much sedative can lead to a fatal overdose. Taking too much of a stimulant drug can lead to over-exhaustion, panic attacks or even in extreme cases, psychotic behaviour.

How often the drug is taken

The more often a drug is taken, the greater the effect and risks. With some drugs a tolerance can develop such that more needs to be taken in order to keep getting an effect. This can be dangerous if heavy use is followed by a period of non-use. This will lead to a drop in tolerance levels, so if the user then restarts at the same level there is a serious risk of overdose. A number of people have fatally overdosed in this way, particularly after coming out of prison. (Not all drugs produce tolerance. LSD has its unique own safeguard against tolerance: if it is taken too frequently it just stops working. No matter how much is taken, there will be no effect at all.)

Adulterated drugs

Some illegal drugs, especially in powder or pill form, have bulking agents and/or other adulterants in them. These can change the effect of the drugs. On rare occasions the adulterants can be dangerous themselves. It is often difficult to know exactly what is contained in a powder or pill.

Drug mixtures

Combining drugs can produce unpredictable and sometimes dangerous effects. In particular, mixtures of sedative drugs can be very dangerous. Many reported drug overdoses involve mixtures of sedatives. Very often one of the drugs involved is alcohol.

How a drug is taken

The method of use will influence the effect that the drug has. Injecting drugs produces a very quick and intense effect. Snorting, inhaling or smoking drugs can also have a quick but slightly less intensive effect. The slowest effect of all is obtained by eating or drinking a drug.

Drug dangers also vary with the method used to take them:

Injecting is particularly risky because it is difficult to know how much is being taken. Injection also carries the risk of infection by blood-borne diseases if any injecting equipment is shared. The highest profile recently has been given to HIV, the virus that leads to AIDS, but there are also risks from hepatitis B and C, very serious blood-borne diseases. Indeed the risk of contracting hepatitis is usually greater than getting HIV because the hepatitis virus survives outside the body longer than the HIV virus.

Eating or drinking a drug can be risky if a lot is taken in one go. The effects tend to be slow but once they come on it is too late to do anything about it. Examples are drinking too much alcohol in a short space of time or eating a lump of cannabis. In both cases people can feel suddenly very drunk or stoned and become very disorientated and/or nauseous.

Snorting drugs like amphetamine or cocaine powder up the nose on a regular basis can lead to damage to the nasal membranes, although this risk has probably been exaggerated.

Inhaling solvents such as glues, gases and aerosols can vary in danger. Squirting solvents into a large plastic bag and then placing the bag over the head has led to death by suffocation. Squirting aerosols or butane straight down the throat has led to deaths through freezing of the airways. Squirting on to a rag or small bag then inhaling is not as dangerous.

Smoking a drug can be a less dangerous method of use than the alternatives, although regular use can damage the respiratory system, especially if the drug is smoked with tobacco, as is often the case with cannabis. Some people have argued that the most dangerous thing about cannabis is the tobacco it is often smoked with.

Injecting drugs, hepatitis, HIV and AIDS

Some users who inject drugs share their 'works' with other users. Tiny traces of blood left in the syringe, on the needle or on other equipment used to make injection possible can carry the HIV virus, hepatitis and other blood-borne infections. Some drug users have passed diseases to each other in this way.

Over 3,000 people in the UK have become HIV positive in this way. Of these people, over 850 had developed AIDS and many have died. The UK figures are small compared to some other countries. In New York alone there are an estimated 100,000 drug users who have become HIV positive through sharing works. More than 5,000 of these have already died from AIDS.

The rates of HIV infection amongst injecting drug users vary widely in different parts of the UK. In Liverpool it is very low. In London it is higher, but the highest of all has been Edinburgh. This probably has something to do with the fact that Liverpool got off the mark early with widespread needle exchange schemes whereas this happened much later in Edinburgh.

In addition to the risk of HIV, drug injectors face the possibility of contracting other blood-borne diseases if they share injecting equipment. Hepatitis B and C are serious diseases that damage the liver and are easier to contract than HIV. This is because the hepatitis virus tends to survive longer outside the body than the HIV virus.

There is a tendency to assume that all of these people are injecting heroin. Many of them will have used heroin, but in some areas other opioid-type drugs are injected as well as tranquillisers such as Temazepam. Amphetamine injecting is quite common in some areas, and in others, such as South Wales, possibly more prevalent than injecting heroin. Cocaine is also sometimes injected and there has been an increase recently in the number of people who inject steroids.

It does not matter which drug is being injected from a hepatitis or HIV risk point of view. All sharing of injection equipment is high risk with regard to blood-borne infections such as hepatitis and HIV, no matter which drug is in the syringe.

The best way to reduce the risk of getting hepatitis or HIV in this way is not to use drugs in the first place. For those who do choose to use drugs the message should be: 'Don't inject.' And for those who will inject, the message must be: 'For heaven's sake, don't share injecting equipment.'

Drug injectors should be encouraged to use the needle exchange schemes which have now been established in most parts of the country as part of the battle against hepatitis, HIV and AIDS. Clean injection equipment is now available free of charge for all drug injectors to help them avoid becoming infected with these viruses or infecting others.

The person

The effects and dangers of drugs are influenced by more than the drugs themselves. Personal factors involving the person who is using the drugs can be just as important as the drugs being used. The drug experience and the expectations of the user are important. Many young people experimenting with drugs for the first time will be unsure about what to do, how much to take, how to take it or what to expect. This ignorance and lack of experience can itself be dangerous.

The effects of drugs and how to get them are learned over time. The first time people use drugs they often find either nothing much happens or they feel sick. This may have happened to you with your first cigarette or drink of alcohol. It is often the same for first use of any drug. Some experimenters decide never to use again but others carry on. Over time they learn how to do it best, what to expect and how to enjoy it most.

The mental and psychological state of the drug user is very important. The mood people are in when they take drugs influences the effects and dangers of drug use. If they are anxious, depressed or unstable, they are more likely to have disturbing experiences when using drugs and less likely to take care. They can become more anxious and disorientated, possibly aggressive, 'freak out' and do crazy things or take too much. In general someone who is happy and stable is more likely to use more carefully and not be so badly affected.

Other things about the drug user that may affect their experience of drug use are:

- Any *physical health problems* like heart disease, high blood pressure, epilepsy, diabetes, asthma or liver problems could make drug use more dangerous. In turn, the drug use could possibly make the health problem worse.
- The drug user's *energy levels at the time of consuming drugs* can also be important. If they are tired at the time of use then the drug may have a different or more extreme effect than if they are fresh and full of energy.
- If the user has a low *body weight* the same amount of drugs may affect them more than they would heavier people. Also people who have an eating disorder like anorexia or bulimia can find that drug use makes it even worse. Cigarettes, amphetamine and ecstasy are all appetite suppressants and have been connected with eating disorders, especially in young women.
- *Males and females* can experience drugs in different ways. This is both because of their different physical make-up and the different way people view male and female drug use. On average women are of smaller body weight than men, have smaller livers as a proportion of body weight and a greater proportion of body fat. This means that, generally speaking, the same amount of drugs will have a greater effect on a woman than on a man. (Obviously this will not apply with a much larger than average woman or a much smaller than average man.)

The effects and risks of drug use are also influenced by attitudes towards men and women taking drugs. Women are often seen as doubly bad if they take drugs: they are bad for taking drugs because it is often viewed as not feminine and, especially if they are mothers, their drug use is seen as a betrayal of this role. Male drug users, even if they are fathers, are not often seen in the same way.

This also spills over to the way pregnant women who use drugs are viewed. Many drugs including alcohol and nicotine can cross the placenta and adversely affect an unborn child. This is especially the case with heavy, regular drug use during pregnancy. Possible effects include increased risk of miscarriage, low birth weight, developmental problems and foetal distress. These problems vary from drug to drug and can also be influenced by many other things including diet, housing conditions, levels of stress and support and medical help. Drug use needs to be kept in perspective. There have been sensationalised stories in the media about 'newborn heroin addicts' or 'crack babies'. The extent to which drug use can affect an unborn child has sometimes been exaggerated. This does not help pregnant women or encourage them to seek medical help.

The environment or setting

The location of drug use can affect the risks. Some youngsters take drugs in out-of-the-way places that are particularly dangerous – on canal banks, near motorways, in derelict buildings, etc. Accidents are much more likely in these places, especially if the user is intoxicated. Also, if anything does go wrong, it is unlikely help will be at hand or that an ambulance could easily be called.

Even if the setting is not in itself inherently dangerous there may be other types of risks associated with the place of use. Using drugs or taking them into school has led to substantial numbers of young people being expelled, often with drastic effects on their future careers.

What people are doing whilst they are using drugs can be an extra risk. Driving a car, riding a motorbike or bicycle or operating machinery whilst on drugs will greatly increase the risk of accidents. Also, drug use can lower inhibitions, which may lead to a greater likelihood of getting into sexual situations whilst under the influence. Avoiding intercourse or practising safe sex – i.e. by using condoms – will be much more difficult if the person concerned is intoxicated. The risks of unwanted pregnancy, HIV and other sexually transmitted diseases are probably increased if young people have sex whilst high on alcohol or drugs. A survey in Liverpool suggested that as many as a third of all sexual encounters by young people under 20 took place whilst under the influence. (For more about the interaction between drug use and sex, see 'What about drugs and sex?', page 56.)

Another danger is that of young people over-exerting themselves when using ecstasy. Ecstasy gives a buzz of energy and is often used in clubs whilst dancing non-stop for long periods.

Sometimes young people have danced for hours without a break in hot, crowded environments, thereby running the risk of becoming dehydrated and getting heat exhaustion. This can be very dangerous and has led to a small number of deaths. 'Chillin' out' – having a break from dancing, cooling off and drinking enough water or fruit juice to replace that lost through sweating (not alcohol as it further dehydrates the user) – reduces these risks. Drinking too much water can, in itself, be dangerous. Sipping a maximum of a pint of water an hour is now recommended for those using 'dance drugs'. Salt depletion can also be a problem for those drinking lots of water so it is also a good idea to eat salty snacks whilst dancing and drinking water.

In conclusion

To understand fully how drugs affect young people and what the risks and dangers are, you will need to think about the drug, the person and the environment as described above. To do this you will need to be able to communicate openly and honestly with your youngster – something we look at in Part II of this book.

7: What does the law say?

The laws covering the use of controlled ('illegal') drugs, as well as those covering 'legal' drugs like alcohol and cigarettes, are complicated. It might help to start by saying what we mean by controlled drugs.

Controlled drugs

The main law covering the use of mood-altering drugs in the UK is the Misuse of Drugs Act. This law controls the possession, supply and production of street drugs like heroin, cocaine and crack, cannabis, amphetamine, ecstasy and LSD. Drugs can also be controlled by the Medicines Act, which affects a wider range of drugs but is aimed more at the manufacture and supply of medicines than the street use of drugs. Drugs controlled by either of these two laws are known as 'controlled drugs'.

There are other laws covering the sale of legal drugs such as alcohol, tobacco and some substances such as solvents, as well as laws covering drunken driving and driving whilst under the influence of drink or drugs.

Before you look through our notes on drug laws, test how much you already know. Have a go at the following quiz.

DRUG LAWS QUIZ

Are these people breaking the law? Answer yes or no.

1. Two 15-year-olds go into a pub by themselves.
2. A mother finds some ecstasy tablets in her daughter's bedroom. According to the father, the law says they have to call the police and hand over the drugs. The mother decides to flush the tablets down the toilet and not tell anyone.
3. A parent allows their 17-year-old to smoke cannabis in the house.
4. A mother has tranquillisers on prescription. She gives a couple to her son on the morning of his driving test as he is so nervous.
5. A nine-year-old sniffs from aerosols in a local park.
6. Three 16-year-olds go into a field and pick and eat magic mushrooms.
7. A shopkeeper sells cigarettes to a 12-year-old.
8. An 18-year-old has a number of syringes.
9. Someone offers to get some heroin for a friend but none is available.
10. A parent drinks three pints of lager in quick succession, hops in their car and drives home.

Answers on page 66.

The Misuse of Drugs Act (MDA)

This law makes the possession, supply, cultivation and manufacture of certain drugs illegal. The drugs it controls are divided into three classes: A, B and C. This law acts as if the Class A drugs are the most dangerous, Class B next most dangerous and Class C least dangerous. The penalties are graded so that the highest penalties are given for offences involving the Class A drugs. A short list of the best known drugs in each class is given below. (For full lists you will need to see a copy of the Act, which you can get from your local branch of Her Majesty's Stationery Office (HMSO). Look up your nearest one in your telephone book. Every major city has one.)

- **Class A drugs** include: cannabis oil, cocaine, crack, ecstasy, heroin, LSD, methadone, morphine, PCP (phencyclidine), processed magic mushrooms and any Class B drug which is prepared for injection.
- **Class B drugs** include: amphetamine, barbiturates, cannabis (in resin and herbal form), codeine, di-hydrocodeine pain-killers (DF 118).
- **Class C drugs** include: tranquillisers (such as Ativan, Librium, Temazepam and Valium), steroids and some minor amphetamine-type drugs.

There are a range of offences under the Act, covering:

- Possession – having a small quantity of a drug in your possession for personal use.
- Possession with intent to supply – having a larger amount of a drug in your possession possibly split up into smaller packages ready for supply.
- Supply or attempting to supply – whether money changes hands or not.
- Production, cultivation or manufacture.
- Import and export.
- Allowing premises to be used for consumption (of some controlled drugs), supply, cultivation, manufacture, etc.

The law is complicated by the fact that some drugs can legally be in someone's possession if they have a prescription for them from a doctor. Methadone, morphine, heroin and all the Class B drugs recorded above, except cannabis, can all be legally prescribed in this way.

The distinction between possession, possession with the intent to supply and actually supplying drugs is not always clear. For example, some young people have gone out to buy relatively small amounts of drugs for friends, using their friend's money and without making any profit, only to be caught by the police and charged with supplying drugs. An example could be a young person who buys 4 LSD 'tabs' at £2.50 each. They could be prosecuted for supplying a Class A drug. This could result in a prison sentence and/or a large fine.

The last offence – allowing premises to be used – is very important for parents to understand. It is illegal for you to allow your children to smoke cannabis or opium, but not to use other controlled drugs, in your home. It is illegal for you to allow your home to be used for growing cannabis plants or for the supply of any controlled drug. In a recent case a mother allowed her teenagers to smoke cannabis in the family home because she feared they would otherwise do it on the streets and felt that would be more dangerous. The police found out and the mother was prosecuted and given a suspended jail sentence. She also nearly lost the tenancy on her council house as the local council had a policy of evicting people who had been prosecuted for allowing their homes to be used for drug use or for supplying controlled drugs.

The penalties under the Misuse of Drugs Act depend on the class of the drug concerned. The maximum penalties for possession and supply are:

	Possession	*Supply*
Class A	7 years and/or a fine	Life imprisonment and a fine
Class B	5 years and/or a fine	14 years and a fine
Class C	2 years and/or a fine	5 years and a fine

These maximum penalties can only be imposed by a Crown Court with a judge and jury. The magistrates' courts have maximum sentences of six months imprisonment and a fine of no more than £5,000. The actual sentence given will depend on the circumstances of each case. This includes: the drug involved and the amount, the type of offence (supply is nearly always punished more severely than possession), previous criminal record and the circumstances of the individual involved (such as whether they are in sole charge of children). In addition judges and magistrates decide penalties and they have quite a lot of discretion about the sentences they give when someone is found guilty of a drug offence. Some are quite lenient but some are quite severe. In reality the type of sentence given for a similar offence can vary a lot in different parts of the country.

In practice a first offence of possession, particularly of a Class

B drug like cannabis, might not even result in a prosecution and so will not reach court. Many police forces caution young people in such circumstances. This involves a stiff talking to by a senior police officer but does not count as a criminal conviction. However, a caution is recorded by the police and is taken into account if the offence occurs again. Police forces in different areas vary in the extent to which they use cautioning but there has been a definite national trend towards cautioning for first possession offences in recent years. Despite this some forces will still prosecute for first offences of small amounts of drugs like cannabis.

In 1995 over 93,000 people in the UK were found guilty or cautioned for drug offences, almost double the number for 1991. 35 per cent of them were under 21 years old. Of these 93,000 people over half were dealt with by cautioning and over 80 per cent of the cases involved cannabis.

The Medicines Act

The 1968 Medicines Act governs the manufacture and supply of medicines and its enforcement rarely affects the public. It can, however, be used to prosecute people for selling certain medicines. Penalties are usually less severe than under the Misuse of Drugs Act.

The law on specific drugs

Alcohol

Despite being the world's second biggest killer drug (after tobacco) alcohol is not controlled under the Misuse of Drugs Act. The laws allow a 14-year-old to go into licensed premises such as a pub, but not to drink alcohol. A 16-year-old can legally buy and consume beer, port, cider or Perry (but not spirits) if they are having a meal in an area set aside for that purpose. It is not illegal for under-18s to drink alcohol away from licensed premises unless they are under 5 years of age. It is an offence for a licensed vendor to knowingly sell alcohol to an under 18-year-old. The police now have powers to confiscate alcohol from under-18s who are drinking on the streets. Some cities have also passed by-laws making it an offence for people of any age to drink on the streets.

Ketamine

Ketamine has recently found its way on to the drug scene in a limited way. It is not yet controlled under the Misuse of Drugs Act, although it has been suggested for inclusion. It is controlled under the Medicines Act, so although it is not illegal to possess or use the drug it is illegal to sell or supply it to someone else.

Magic mushrooms

Magic mushrooms grow wild all over the country in autumn. They are not controlled under the Misuse of Drugs Act in their natural state, but they do contain a chemical (psilocin) which is a Class A drug. This means that in their raw state they are not controlled but if prepared in any way – even just by drying them out, cooking with them or making them into a tea – they could be viewed as preparations of the controlled drug and become Class A.

Nitrites (poppers/liquid gold)

They are widely available in joke and sex shops, in clubs, some tobacconists and some young people's clothes and record shops. They have even been sold openly over the bar in pubs and clubs. The legal status of nitrites is complex. Amyl nitrite is controlled under pharmacy legislation and should not be available but prosecutions for supply are so far rare. Butyl nitrite – which is the drug actually found in almost all of the nitrites used by young people – is not legally controlled at all. There have been attempts to use the 'Sale of Intoxicating Substances Act' by local trading standards officers to prohibit sales of all nitrites to under-18s but so far they have not been successful. They are still widely available.

Over-the-counter (OTC) medicines

There are many over-the-counter medicines that can be bought from a chemist without a prescription and used for their intoxicating effect. They include cough medicines that contain opioids, pain killers used for period pains and severe headaches, travel sickness pills and other medicines that can have sedative, stimulant or hallucinogenic properties.

Solvents, glues and gases

These are not controlled under the Misuse of Drugs Act. There are so many of them on general sale for quite legitimate purposes that it would be impossible legally to ban them. In England and Wales it is an offence for a shopkeeper to sell such substances to an under 18-year-old, if they know they are likely to be used for intoxicating purposes. There is also the possibility that young people under the influence might be charged with public order offences if they are making a nuisance of themselves.

Steroids

Steroids have been recently brought under the Misuse of Drugs Act as Class C drugs but the possession offence is waived. They can only legally be sold by a pharmacist and only legally obtained on prescription from a doctor. It is illegal to supply them to another person but not illegal to be in possession of them for personal use. Prosecutions are so far rare.

Tobacco

It is not illegal to possess or use tobacco or supply it to another person at no charge. It is only illegal for a vendor to knowingly sell tobacco products to an under-16. The government is considering changing the age limit to 18 to bring it in line with alcohol. It is not illegal for an under-16 to smoke cigarettes.

Tranquillisers

These are Class C drugs under the Misuse of Drugs Act but the possession offence does not apply if the drugs are in the form of a medicine. It is not an offence to be in possession of most tranquillisers in their medicinal/tablet form without a prescription. It is an offence to supply them to another person, even if they have been obtained by prescription in the first place. This applies whether or not any money changes hands. For example, if a parent has tranquillisers on prescription from a doctor and gives their teenager a few to calm them down, the parent but not the teenager, is breaking the law. The only exception is Temazepam (a tranquilliser which is now popular with some drug users) for which there is now a possession offence unless the drug has been supplied for the person in possession – on a doctor's prescription.

8: What do different drugs look like?

Imagine that you have come across a powder, some pills or a strange looking substance in your youngster's bedroom. What is it? Is it a drug and if so which? Understandably a lot of parents want to know what different drugs look like. The problem is – it's not that simple.

Take cannabis, for example. Cannabis comes from a plant – *Cannabis sativa*. The plant can be bushy and/or very tall – three to four feet in the UK, up to 10 feet high or more in a hot country. Most often you will see cannabis as a block of resin. This has been processed from the leaves of the plant and made into a block. It can vary in colour from light golden or greenish brown to very dark brown or black. It can feel light, dry and crumbly or heavy, oily and very hard. Both texture and colour can vary between these extremes. Imagine a chicken stock cube but a little harder or at the other extreme – a piece of French chalk but much darker, maybe almost black.

In addition to the resin you might come across herbal cannabis. This is the cannabis leaves dried out and ready to smoke. The colour and texture of the leaves will vary depending upon the exact type of plant and where it has been grown. Imported herbal cannabis will often be different in texture and colour from home grown. Appearances vary so much that even experienced users have occasionally been caught out buying dried everyday herbs and grasses believing them to be cannabis. Finally, you might come across cannabis oil. This is extracted from the resin and is the strongest concentration of cannabis found in the UK. It is very dark and oily, looking a bit like treacle.

Cannabis has a very distinctive smell, which once you have smelled it, you are unlikely to forget. But if you have not smelled it yet – well, smells are very difficult to describe. Try and describe the smell of garlic to someone who doesn't know what it is. It's almost impossible – garlic smells like . . . garlic, and that's all there is to it. And cannabis? Well, it smells like . . . cannabis. Complicated isn't it? And cannabis is much easier for a novice to recognise than many other drugs.

Powders

Some drugs, such as amphetamine, cocaine and heroin, come in powder form. They can vary in colour depending on where, when and how they have been processed. All of the 'laboratories' making these drugs are highly illegal and none are subject to quality control. Each batch may be different from the last. Often bulking agents are mixed in to add to the volume although contrary to popular belief they are only very rarely more harmful than the drug they are being added to.

The colour and consistency will vary enormously. Heroin, for example, can be white, grey, cream coloured, brownish and all shades in between. Cocaine is usually a white crystalline powder but it can also vary in colour and consistency. Amphetamine can be a white, grey or even pink powder. Even regular users get ripped off sometimes buying powdered milk or laxatives dressed up to look like heroin or cocaine. There are also medicines and many household products which are powders and can easily be mistaken for drugs.

Tablets and capsules

Identifying drugs is even harder when they are in tablet or capsule form. There are several thousands of different medicines that come in these forms. Many of these have some sedative, stimulant or hallucinogenic property. Some of these are available over-the-counter from chemists or even with some popular drugs from supermarkets. There are also 'home-made' tablets and capsules and even capsules used for illegal drugs which have been recycled from legitimate medical drug use. All of this makes it very difficult to distinguish drugs such as amphetamines, ecstasy, tranquillisers or steroids.

LSD

LSD can come in a variety of forms. Often it is in the form of small, impregnated squares of blotting paper. Some of these are overprinted to look like the transfers you see young children playing with. In some areas there have been drug scares when parents have thought local children playing with transfers might be using LSD. It has not been LSD and it is unlikely that young children would come into contact with it. However, the confusion arose because the everyday transfers looked like LSD squares. Many of the street names for the drug are derived from the printed picture or appearance – e.g. strawberries, penguins, rainbows, Gorbachovs, ferns, etc. LSD can also be dripped on to sugar cubes or processed with sugar into mini tablets. These are home-made and come in all sorts of shapes such as stars, diamonds, etc.

Drug paraphernalia

These are the things drug users will sometimes have about them to help them use drugs. Take care with these, as many of them have legitimate uses that have nothing to do with drugs.

Cannabis is usually smoked. In order to make up cannabis cigarettes ('joints') there will be cigarette papers (some of normal length and some larger) and often small, rolled-up tubes of cardboard for the filter tip or 'roach'. A wide variety of pipes are also used to smoke cannabis or more elaborate hubble-bubble pipes to draw the smoke through water thus cooling it. The cannabis will sometimes be supplied in little self-sealing plastic bags or in twists of silver foil or cling film.

Smoking heroin is often done by 'chasing the dragon'. This involves heating the powder up to the point at which it vaporises or gives off smoke that is then drawn up into the mouth or nose through a straw or rolled-up paper tube. The powder will be put on to tinfoil or perhaps a metal spoon so that a match or cigarette lighter can be used from below. These items may be found in a burnt or discoloured state.

Drugs prepared for injection must be made into a solution that will go through a syringe. The paraphernalia can include: needles and syringes, water, lemon juice, citric acid, cigarette filter tips or pieces of tampon (to trap any chalk from crushed tablets in solution), a rubber tube or strap to act as tourniquet when preparing the veins to receive the needle and metal bottle tops and spoons or similar to act as a 'cooker' for the water.

Other items associated with drug use include:

- foil containers or cup shapes made from silver foil
- metal tins
- pill boxes
- plastic, cellophane or metal foil wrappers

- small plastic or glass vials or bottles
- twists of paper
- straws
- sugar lumps
- spent matches
- plastic bags with traces of glue
- butane gas cylinders
- stamps, stickers, transfers
- shredded or home-made cigarettes
- torn cigarette packets or pieces of card

Warning

Given the everyday objects listed above and how difficult it can be to recognise different drugs for sure, we cannot finish this part of the book without stressing the following. If you do find something suspicious and think it could be associated with drug use ask your youngster, but do it in a low key way.

For advice on what to actually do if you find something you think is suspicious see Part III, 'Coping in a crisis', page 109. See also the drug education resources for parents listed on page 157 which include a card game, video and computer programme which show pictures of drugs.

9: How can you tell if your youngster is using drugs?

As a parent you will want to know if your youngster is using drugs. What should you be looking out for? One way would to find drug paraphernalia as described above. There are also lists of signs and symptoms that have been put together to try to help parents know what changes in behaviour or appearance to look out for in their youngsters. Is it possible to look through these lists, keep an eye on your youngsters and spot the telltale signs of drug use? Unfortunately, it is not always that easy.

Signs and symptoms

Below is an extract from *Drug Misuse and the Young: A Guide for the Education Service,* a pamphlet published by the Department for Education in 1992 (reproduced with the permission of the Controller of Her Majesty's Stationery Office). It aims to help teachers to recognise the signs of drug use in young people.

Warning signs in individuals

- Decline in performance in schoolwork or youth club activities.
- Changes in attendance and being unwilling to take part in school or youth club group activities.
- Unusual outbreaks of temper, marked swings of moods, restlessness or irritability.
- Reports from parents that more time is being spent away from home, possibly with new friends or with friends in older age groups.
- Excessive spending or borrowing of money.
- Stealing money or goods.
- Excessive tiredness without obvious cause.
- No interest in physical appearance.
- Sores or rashes, especially on the mouth or nose.
- Lack of appetite.
- Heavy use of scents, colognes etc. to disguise the smell of drugs.
- Wearing sunglasses at inappropriate times (to hide dilated or constricted pupils).

Warning signs in groups

- Regular absence on certain days (e.g. the day young people receive state benefits).
- Keeping at a distance from other pupils, students or youth club members, away from supervision points (e.g. groups who frequently gather near the gate of a school playground or sports field).
- Being the subject of rumours about drug taking.
- Talking to strangers on or near the premises.
- Stealing which appears to be the work of several individuals rather than one person (e.g. perhaps to shoplift solvents).
- Use of drug takers' slang.

- Exchanging money or other objects in unusual circumstances.
- Associating briefly with one person who is much older and not normally part of the peer group.

The problem is that many of the listed signs and symptoms are normal aspects of adolescent behaviour. All of them could be due to things other than drug use. Most of the time using a drug does not result in clear signs and symptoms unless you happen to be with the user whilst they are actually intoxicated. Think about alcohol for a moment. You cannot tell if someone uses alcohol just by looking at them. Perhaps you could smell alcohol on their breath if they had just had a drink. If they were drunk you probably would know. Maybe if they were a really heavy drinker they might have a red face. But most of the time you would not be able to tell. It is the same with other drugs. If they are any use at all the lists of signs and symptoms usually only apply to the very heavy and chaotic users. These are only a small minority. Most young people use drugs occasionally and do not fall into this category.

Drug effects are complex. The same drug can produce different effects on different people. The same drug can even produce different effects on the same person at different times depending on their mood, as explained earlier (see page 39). So predicting drug use by trying to spot its effects can be an unreliable business. What if you get it wrong? Young people will resent being accused of things they have not done. The 'signs' may be nothing more than unconfirmed rumours and your imagination.

Drug testing

Drug testing is becoming more widespread in industry and in sport. Some schools, particularly prestigious public schools, have also begun drug testing their students. And now some companies are advertising drug testing kits which parents can buy.

There are different types of tests. Blood tests are expensive, require medical intervention and often involve a sample being sent to a laboratory for testing. The most commonly used test involves urine but again this usually involves samples being sent to a laboratory for analysis. Recently hair testing has been introduced and kits for parents to use at home have been on sale.

Parents should think very carefully before attempting to drug test their own children or agreeing to a school doing it. There are a lot of problems involved in drug testing young people including:

- The results – particularly from home testing kits – are not always accurate. There can be false positives (a positive result where there is no drug use) and false negatives (a negative result where there has been drug use).
- If medicines have been taken they may give a positive test. For example, some cold remedies and cough syrups could produce positive results for opioids and/or amphetamine.
- Timing. Whilst hair tests can detect drug use going back over a longish period of time – depending on the length of the hair tested – urine tests do not.
- Urine tests may only detect recent use. The approximate detection periods are:
  - alcohol   12–24 hours
  - amphetamine   2–4 days
  - cannabis   2–7 days but up to one month for regular users
  - cocaine/crack   12 hours–3 days
  - ecstasy   2–4 days
  - heroin   1–2 days
  - LSD   2–3 days
- Hair tests are not as reliable as urine testing unless done in a competent laboratory.
- Hair testing may show up small traces of drugs such as cannabis or crack cocaine which have been absorbed through the smoke in the air, for example at a party, where others have been smoking drugs even if the person concerned has had none of the drug.
- Some types of shampoo and colourant may remove drugs from the hair.
- Testing young people destroys trust and can make them understandably resentful. It can destroy any possibility of open and honest communication and may prevent young people, who are having problems, from seeking help.

In conclusion

There are many parallels in this chapter with the previous section on what drugs look like. In both cases there is no substitute for talking and listening to your youngsters. If you think they are behaving oddly and you are worried about the possibility of drug use, say so. Tell them about your concerns without going over the top. Listen carefully to what they have to say. The key is communication with your youngster (see Part II for ideas on how to achieve good communication). Parents and youngsters talking together can break through the mystique of drug use. Lists of signs and symptoms and drug testing have little value in helping that communication process.

10: What about drugs and sex?

N.B. This part is about sex and drugs. For information about the risks of HIV, the virus that leads to AIDS, from injecting drugs see 'What effects do drugs have and what are the dangers?', page 34.

Sex 'n' drugs 'n' rock 'n' roll. That was what the 1960s were supposed to be about. In the 1990s, electronic dance music has taken over from rock 'n' roll but the sex and drugs are still there. Alcohol is the drug most commonly used to overcome inhibitions and to help people relax. Having loosened up in the bar, many young people will loosen up on the dance floor and hope to loosen up later in bed or in the back seat of someone's car.

One problem arising from this is that safe sex is often forgotten about once a few drinks are taken. It is difficult to stay in control, avoid unprotected intercourse or to use condoms if you are out of your head. And of course for many young people it is not just the result of alcohol. Other drugs and sex often go together.

A survey in Liverpool showed that about 30 per cent of all the young people asked – over 1,000 – reported recently having sex under the influence of drink or drugs. Of these about a third said that it was sex that would not have taken place if they had not been intoxicated. Whenever sexual intercourse takes place there are risks both of unwanted pregnancy and of sexually transmitted viruses such as HIV (the virus which leads to AIDS) and hepatitis as well as syphilis, gonorrhoea and chlamydia.

Because there are so many myths about drugs and sex it is worth noting what is known for each main drug.

Amphetamines

These are widely used as a 'dance drug' by young people. They have been claimed to prevent premature ejaculation and prolong sexual interest in both males and females but they can reduce the likelihood of either sex achieving an orgasm. Sometimes it is said that prolonged use of amphetamines will reduce the size of a man's erect penis.

Caffeine and tobacco

These popular legal drugs have their part to play in the game of sex, although it is more in the rituals before and after than in the act itself. The post-coital cigarette is not as popular as it once was and the idea of making love to someone who has a fag in their mouth must be one of life's great turn-offs. Caffeine puts in an appearance at an earlier stage in the mating game, as in, 'Are you coming back for a coffee?'

Cannabis

Using cannabis produces a mellowing effect that some users say can enhance sexual pleasure. The ways in which perception is changed by the drug can increase the intensity of sexual pleasure if users learn to interpret the effects that way. Taking larger doses of cannabis can produce nausea, diarrhoea or vomiting, which will not help sexual attractiveness! Cannabis use can also result in short-term memory loss, making remembering to practise safer sex – or even where the condoms are – more difficult.

Cocaine and crack

These drugs can make people feel more powerful and aggressive. However, they can also make it difficult for men to get an erection and for women to have an orgasm. Crack use has also been identified with prostitution in some areas although it is difficult to know which comes first.

Ecstasy

This is also a dance drug and has been described as 'the love drug' or sometimes 'the hug drug'. This is because users often report that they lose any feelings of anger or hostility and are taken over by serene feelings of well being and affection. The experience tends to enhance feelings of sexual pleasure rather than increase libido. As with amphetamines, ecstasy may also inhibit orgasm and male erection. There is debate about whether its use will increase the risk of unsafe sex or decrease it.

Heroin, other opioids and tranquillisers

These drugs are all sedatives and tend to reduce interest in sex. They will probably lead to an individual going more into themselves than into interaction with others. There have been claims that heavy use of sedatives by women makes them more vulnerable to sexual abuse and exploitation. There is also clear evidence of high levels of sedative use amongst prostitutes, although the cause–effect relationship is not clear. Are the prostitutes selling themselves to raise money for drugs or using drugs to block out the unpleasantness of prostitution? Probably both are true.

The media has branded one particular tranquilliser – Rohypnol – as 'the date rape drug'. It has been alleged that this drug has been slipped into the drinks of young women who either pass out or experience short-term memory loss and are then vulnerable to sexual exploitation and rape. To the extent to which this has actually happened, it echoes in an even more unpleasant form, the tendency of some men to try to get women drunk in order to exploit them sexually. It also raises some difficult issues for the media. To what extent does coverage of this issue put it into the minds of some men who are not even aware that tranquillisers could have such an effect?

LSD and magic mushrooms

In the 1990s LSD has made a comeback as another dance drug. Its effects are unpredictable. In some individuals LSD use will lower sexual interest as the user goes off into their own inner world. In others the loss of inhibitions that accompanies the drug use will enhance sexual pleasure. Magic mushrooms have similar effects to LSD, although milder.

Nitrites

Nitrites (poppers, rush, liquid gold etc.) have a history of being used in clubs and pubs, particularly by gay men, to increase sexual desire and pleasure, often at the moment of orgasm. More recently they have come into common use amongst young people as dance drugs.

Steroids

These are a group of hormones that occur naturally in the body and are involved in the working of the reproductive organs. The main male hormone is testosterone. Steroids are often taken to enhance athletic performance or for 'body building'. Because they interact with the body's own hormones they can have complex effects on sexual functioning. In men steroid use can lower sperm count. Interest in sex may be increased at first, but with further use of steroids will be diminished. There are reports of aggression and sexual violence by men using large amounts of steroids. There are also reports of 'testicular atrophy' (shrinking) amongst regular male users. Women using steroids may experience increased sex drive, irregular periods and an enlarged clitoris. There are also reports of women decreasing in breast size and developing facial hair and sometimes a deepening of the voice. These effects seem to be irreversible.

In conclusion

What can parents do about drugs and sex? It will help to brief yourself about the ways in which sex and drugs might interact. In addition to concerns about drug use, many parents will also be concerned about the risks of sex at too early an age, sexually transmitted diseases and unwanted pregnancy. By being prepared to discuss these matters openly with your children you will be in the best position to help them to reduce these risks.

11: What kind of help is available?

There are different kinds of help available for people who have problems with drugs or need advice and information. 'Know where and how to get help in your area', page 98, explains what you need to do to get help, and helping organisations are listed in Appendix II, page 154. Below are described the different types of help that are available across the UK. A good way to find out about drug services in your area is to call the National Drugs Helpline on 0800 77 66 00. They give free, confidential telephone advice 24 hours a day and should also be able to give you details of services in your area.

Until recently few specialist drug organisations worked with young people under the age of 16, usually focusing on the 18-plus age range, especially those who inject drugs like heroin. This is gradually changing and whilst some still only see under-16s with parental consent, many are now offering services to young people sometimes without requiring parental consent.

Family doctors

The family doctor or GP is the cornerstone of health services in the UK. GPs should be able to offer you help and advice on drug problems as on other family health issues. They should be able to give you or your youngster advice, sometimes prescribe substitute drugs (see Substitute prescribing pp. 61–2) and certainly should have information on local specialist services.

Sadly, however, some family doctors are simply not up to scratch when it comes to dealing with drug issues. They may have been trained before drug problems became widespread in the UK and even today GP training does not adequately deal with how to work with drug users. Despite this, many GPs have made the effort to inform themselves and can provide an excellent service. Do not be too surprised though if your GP cannot cope well with drug use. If you wish, you can always change your GP or, if you are satisfied with their performance in other respects, you might want to go elsewhere for drug advice and support. Fortunately there are other services available in most areas.

Drug advice and counselling agencies

The names of these services vary from area to area. In some areas they are called Community Drug Teams or Drug Advice Services, but often they have names which are drawn from the area they operate in, such as the 'Merseyside Drugs Council'. They offer a range of services both to those using drugs and to their families and friends. The services they offer can include:

- Information about drugs.
- Advice to drug users about drug risks.
- Counselling for drug users and/or their families.
- Syringe exchange.
- Outreach or 'detached' work in the community.
- Support for self-help groups.
- Referral to residential treatment services.

Their services can usually be offered over the telephone as well as seeing people face-to-face. The services usually work on an appointment basis although some will offer a drop-in facility. Most of these services will meet their clients mainly at their project base while others can visit clients in their homes. Some services have doctors who can prescribe substitute drugs.

Hospital-based services

These are usually for people who are heavy, long-term drug users, particularly injecting heroin users. GPs can also offer these prescription services although some are reluctant to do so. The treatments given will vary between different areas. Hospital-based specialist drug services often require a letter of referral from a GP, social worker, probation officer or local drug service. Hospital beds may be available if needed for in-patient detox services (see below) but there is often a waiting list.

Needle/syringe exchange schemes

These are for injecting drug users. They aim to ensure that drug injectors do not have to share injecting equipment. This helps to limit the spread of hepatitis, HIV and AIDS. Some exchange schemes are based within drug advice projects but others operate from chemist shops or hospitals. Some exchange schemes also include outreach workers who meet users in their homes or on

---

Substitute prescribing

Doctors in the UK have always been able to prescribe certain drugs in the treatment of dependence. Up until the 1960s the drugs most widely prescribed were heroin and morphine. The idea behind the system was that if drug users could get a controlled supply of pure and legal drugs they would be unlikely to use street drugs. This would hopefully reduce the health risks from reliance on street drugs and also the need to commit crimes to fund their drug habits. Prescribing of substitute drugs was undertaken as part of detoxification treatment designed to overcome the dependency on drugs or as 'maintenance treatment'. 'Maintenance' aims to stabilise drug users on legal supplies for an extended time period.

In the late 1960s doctors became concerned at the amount of legally prescribed heroin which was finding its way on to the streets and fuelling a so-called 'grey market' in street-level drug use. This concern gave rise to controls in the ways in which substitute drugs could be supplied and to changes in the drugs used. These changes were designed to control the risks of drugs being diverted into street-level use whilst continuing with the core idea of substitute prescription.

Detoxification

Drugs such as methadone are prescribed to help wean users from their dependence on drugs. It is sometimes called 'detox' for short. The process of detox is that of gradual reduction in the dose to make the withdrawal effects less painful. After an initial assessment a judgement is made of the starting dose and a program agreed for the duration of the detox. This can be as short as 10 days or as long as six months. Most detox programs are undertaken 'in the community' and last 30 days or so. In some difficult cases, in-patient detox might be undertaken in specialist hospital settings.

Maintenance

Maintenance prescribing today uses a variety of drugs. The drug most often used is methadone, an opioid which is usually taken orally rather than by injection and which is slower acting than heroin. Although heroin is still used with up to 10 per cent of those who are receiving a maintenance prescription, it can only be prescribed by specialist doctors whilst some other drugs, including methadone, can be prescribed by family doctors. Although maintenance prescribing is still controversial to some people, it has been extensively researched across the world. Solid evidence exists that if it is properly managed it is a very effective treatment in the management of drug dependence. It is now widely used in the UK, the USA, Europe and Australia as well as in some Asian countries.

the streets. They are confidential services. Users do not have to give their name. As well as clean injecting equipment they also offer advice, information and access to health services. See also 'Injecting drugs, hepatitis, HIV and AIDS' on page 38.

Although these are controversial services for some people they have been carefully researched in the UK and have been shown to reduce the risks of HIV infection amongst drug injectors. The UK's commitment to needle exchange schemes and other 'harm reduction' techniques is internationally recognised as the main reason why the UK has avoided a serious epidemic of AIDS amongst drug injectors whilst others countries without such services have suffered big epidemics and many more deaths.

Residential rehabilitation centres

These are residential units often based in large houses either in the countryside or sometimes on the outskirts of large towns and cities. In most cases they operate on a basis of complete abstinence from drugs and alcohol for an extended period of rehabilitation. Although each individual centre has its own unique blend of theory and practice they tend to fall into one of several main categories.

Funding is a problem for most residential units. It is based on payments made either by the individual client or more often by their social services department after an assessment of need and suitability to benefit from the service offered. There are sometimes serious problems finding funding for some clients and in some areas. Funding in all areas is limited and in some areas has run out for the last few months of every financial year.

Therapeutic programmes can run from three months to over a year. Although most therapeutic communities have a substantial turnover of clients in the first month, most of those who stay three months or more will go on to an extended or even indefinite period of abstinence. Research in the USA and the UK has shown that well run therapeutic communities are effective treatments for many drug users including those who might have failed in other treatment systems.

The 'concept' Therapeutic Communities (TCs)

These were based on a personal regrowth concept originally derived from the 'Synanon' communities in the United States. In its original US form, the internal regimes could be quite harsh with residents undergoing sustained verbal and psychological confrontation until they acknowledged their personal responsibility for their life situation.

Once this acknowledgement was achieved the work could begin of gradual regrowth of self and self-respect until the resident was ready to take their place in the world as a responsible and contributing citizen. Whilst a resident of the TC each person would take on physical work programmes and programmes of self-analysis sometimes conducted one-to-one but more often in quite confrontative 'encounter' groups.

The UK 'concept' houses

The UK versions of these 'concept' houses were never as harsh or dogmatic in style as their US counterparts. Over the last ten years and particularly since the AIDS epidemic in the mid 1980s the concept houses have considerably changed their style and most now tailor individual treatment packages for their clients with extensive use of key worker systems. This means that each client has their own key worker rather than all the clients being put through the same programme.

Despite this there is still widespread use of therapeutic groups, and sometimes peer confrontation. These are linked to rigorous work programmes which challenge the individual to take responsibility for themselves and for the well being and comfort of others.

12 step Communities

These are based on the 12 steps to recovery first promoted by the organisation Alcoholics Anonymous (AA). These communities have a similar 'disease model' of addiction to AA and they recommend that their residents continue their 'recovery' after leaving the communities by regular attendance at AA or NA (Narcotics Anonymous) meetings.

The work on the programme will consist of both individual counselling and group psychotherapy with an emphasis on confrontation of destructive and addictive behaviours. Residential programmes rarely last longer than three months. 12 step communities are run by both charitable and 'for profit' agencies. Some of them can be quite expensive, as all the running costs may have to come from client fees.

Christian therapeutic communities

These use a wide variety of methods similar to other communities but also have some religious content. In many of the Christian houses the religious content is muted and optional for the clients but in others the approach is very evangelical with frequent prayer meetings for all residents and staff.

Self-help groups for drug users, parents and families

These exist in many areas. Your local drug advice service should be able to tell you what is available. You can also contact the National Drugs Helpline on 0800 77 66 00 or one of the following national organisations:

- **ADFAM** The national charity for families and friends of drug users. They run a national helpline Tel. 0171 928 8900 in office hours.
- **Families Anonymous** are involved in support groups for parents and families of drug users in different parts of the country. Tel. 0171 498 4680.
- **Narcotics Anonymous** – this is a network of self-help groups for drug users based on the Alcoholics Anonymous approach. They also have a helpline. Tel. 0171 730 0009.
- **Release** runs a 24-hour national helpline specially for people who have been arrested for a drug offence. They also give legal advice to parents. They can be contacted on 0171 603 8654.

Non-specialist young people's advice and counselling services

These types of services exist in some areas. They do not specialise in drugs but they do specialise in working with young people. Local colleges, youth clubs or youth projects sometimes offer similar confidential services for young people.

In conclusion

There are now helping services of many kinds available in different parts of the country. Do find out what is available in your locality (see 'Finding out more about drug use in your area', page 19) and do not feel shy about approaching services if you feel you need them.

Drug laws quiz answers

From page 43.

1. *No*. Young people over 14 are allowed into a pub by themselves so long as they do not buy or consume alcohol.
2. *No*. If you find illegal drugs you do not have to inform the police. You can destroy them yourself. But don't hang on to them or you will be at risk of prosecution for possession of controlled drugs.
3. *Yes*. The parent and the 17-year-old are both breaking the law. It is illegal to allow your home to be used for the smoking of cannabis or opium (but not for use of other controlled drugs like heroin, cocaine, LSD or ecstasy) or to be used for the supply of any controlled drug.
4. *Yes*. She is breaking the law but the son is not. The supply of tranquillisers to another person is illegal under both the Medicines and Misuse of Drugs Act but it is not illegal to use them, with or without a prescription. The exception is Temazepam, see page 48.
5. *No*. It is not illegal to use aerosols, glues or other solvents, at any age. It is only illegal to sell or supply solvents to under-18s knowing that they will use them for intoxication. However, there have been cases of young people being charged with public order offences such as 'Behaviour likely to cause a breach of the peace' after becoming high on glues/solvents in public places.
6. *No*. Magic mushrooms are not illegal to use raw. They are only illegal to use if processed, made into a tea, cooked with, etc. In such a case they are viewed as a controlled drug under the Misuse of Drugs Act.
7. *Yes*. The 12-year-old is not breaking the law but the shopkeeper is. It is not illegal to buy or use cigarettes at any age but it is illegal for a shopkeeper to knowingly sell them to an under 16-year-old.
8. *No*. It is not illegal to possess or use injecting equipment. It depends what drugs are injected. If it is tranquillisers the user is not breaking the law. They might also inject insulin – they might be diabetic. Even if they are injecting heroin it is not the use itself which is illegal, but the possession of heroin, which is controlled under the Misuse of Drugs Act.
9. *Yes*. The person who offered to get the heroin could be prosecuted with conspiring to supply a controlled drug.
10. *Yes (probably)*. The legal limit for drink driving is about two and a half pints for most men and slightly less for most women.

How did you do? If you got fewer than six right you might want to do some research. Have a look through the notes on the Misuse of Drugs Act on pages 43–6 and maybe look up a few of the books recommended in Appendix II, page 156.

Part II
WHAT EVERY PARENT CAN DO: BE PREPARED

1: Be informed – learn facts not myths

'All they say is "Don't do it" or "It'll kill you." We still do it. They don't know what they're talking about.'

– 15-year-old

In order to be prepared, you must first be informed. You don't have to know everything about drugs, but you do need to avoid the many myths and half-truths that surround drug use. This can be difficult because the harm from drug use is often overstated. Sometimes an extreme example is presented as though it is what normally happens every time. Drug issues are often presented on television and in the newspapers in an exaggerated and sensationalised way. Drug users in films and novels are usually sleazy, low-life characters. The vast majority of drug use is totally unlike these stereotypes. In view of this it can be difficult to keep illicit drug use in its proper perspective.

It may help to revise the reasons why young people use drugs. Have a look at the exercise below and see if it helps to sharpen up your understanding.

REASONS WHY YOUNG PEOPLE USE DRUGS

Look through the list below of reasons why someone might use drugs.

1. Drugs are **freely available**.
2. **Everyone** does it.
3. It's the **fashion**.
4. It's **fun**.
5. It makes you **feel good**.
6. It's **exciting**.
7. **Pressure** from other young people.
8. It's a **protest** against society and adults.
9. Out of **boredom**.
10. To try to **block out feelings** of emotional pain or inadequacy.

Now answer the questions that follow. Write down the key words you think fit best.

1. Which of the reasons best explains why:
   a) A 14-year-old experiments with sniffing butane gas with friends.
   b) A 16-year-old locks themselves in their bedroom all day and sniffs three canisters of butane gas.
   c) A 17-year-old smokes cannabis with friends at weekends when it is available.
   d) A 16-year-old takes ecstasy every weekend and goes to all-night clubs with a crowd who also uses.
   e) An 18-year-old chain-smokes and drinks at least six pints of lager a day with mates.
   f) The family doctor has prescribed a 16-year-old tranquillisers after the death of their mother.
   g) A 19-year-old has become dependent on heroin and injects every day.
2. Which of the reasons best explains your own use of drugs (legal and illegal) when you were young?
3. Which of the reasons might apply to your youngster(s) today?

Now ask your youngster to go through the questions with you and discuss your answers with them.

Now have a go at the quiz that follows. It will help you further to sort some of the drug myths from the drug reality.

———————— DRUG MYTHS QUIZ ————————

Work out whether each of the statements below is true or a myth.

Answer true or false:

1. All drug use is dangerous.
2. Illegal drugs are more dangerous than the legal ones.
3. More people die through use of alcohol each year than through heroin.
4. Once they start on cannabis they go on to heroin.
5. Most people who take drugs come to no serious harm.

6. One try of heroin, cocaine or crack and you are 'hooked' for life.
7. Most drug users commit crime to get the money to buy drugs.
8. Only a small number of youngsters try illegal drugs.
9. It is often very difficult to spot if someone is using drugs.
10. Most young people get their drugs from their friends.
11. All illegal drugs come into this country from abroad.
12. Illegal drugs are not always that expensive.
13. Young people take drugs because they mix with the wrong sort.
14. I am a drug taker.
15. If young people knew how dangerous drugs were they wouldn't use them.

Answers on page 105.

Some other things you can do are:

1. Try the quiz with your partner, a friend and/or your youngster.
2. Think about some of the other myths that surround drug use. What are they and why do people believe them? Discuss this with your partner, a friend and/or your youngster. Ask your youngster what drug myths they think parents often believe.
3. Look at the way television, magazines and newspapers report on drug issues. What myths and stereotypes do they use?
4. Learn more by reading and using computers and the Internet (see Appendix II, 'Where to find out more', page 154) or going on local education workshops or courses.

'I know it's true that most young people use drugs without getting into harm. I know it but still find it difficult to bring myself to believe it.'

– Parent

'I have realised that I do know quite a lot about drugs. In the past I was so anxious about it that I couldn't think sensibly or clearly – I sort of forgot what I already knew.'

– Parent

2: Think about your own use of drugs

'I booze regularly, smoke fags and drink gallons of coffee. When I was young I tried speed and smoked cannabis. But basically I don't believe in drugs.'

– Parent

'Drugs are something other people do.' We do not often see our own drug use as being drug use at all. But almost all of us take, or have taken, drugs of one sort or another. Even those of us who are teetotal, don't smoke, never use aspirin or other medicines and don't drink tea, coffee or soft drinks have probably used some of them at some time in the past.

Think about your own drug use – both now and in the past. What has it been like? How does it influence your attitudes towards young people's drug use today? What sort of messages does your own use of drugs (past and present) give to your own youngster(s)?

In order to help you do this, try the following exercise.

——————YOUR OWN DRUG USE——————

Look at the list of drugs below. Then answer the questions. Finally talk through your answers with your partner or a friend.

The drugs

alcohol
amphetamine
aspirin/codeine
cannabis
cocaine/crack
ecstasy
heroin (or other opioid drugs)
LSD
magic mushrooms
poppers (nitrites)
sleeping pills

solvents (glue/gas/aerosols, etc.)
steroids
tea, coffee (caffeine)
tobacco
tranquillisers (Librium, Temazepam, Valium, etc.)

The questions

1. Which drugs have you ever used?
2. Which ones did you try when you were young?
3. Why did you try them?
4. Did you enjoy your use of drugs when you were young? If so, in what ways?
5. Which drugs have you used in the past year?
6. Why do you use them?
7. Overall, has your use of drugs been a good or bad experience?
8. What does this tell you about:
   a) you as a youngster?
   b) your life now?
   c) how drug use might change as people get older?
   d) young people's use of drugs?
   e) the example you set for your youngster?

Drug careers

We all have drug careers. At different stages of our lives our drug use changes. At one time we might be using almost no drugs at all. At another time we might be experimenting with lots of different drugs. At yet another time we might be using just one or two drugs but using them regularly. It depends on what is going on in our lives at the time.

Try plotting a 'Drug Career Graph' for yourself like the one on page 74. Choose one or two drugs you have used over the years. Alcohol is often a good one to start with. Note on the graph how your use of the drug has changed over the years. Then look at the graph and think about what was going on in your life at these different times. What does it tell you about your drug use? What lessons might there be about young people's drug use? Discuss your drug career with a partner or friend and ask them about their drug career.

Drug Career Graph

Very heavy,
every day use ···

Moderate,
regular use ···

Moderate,
occasional use ···

No use
at all ──

Age   5   15   25   35   45   65   75

Explaining your drug use to your youngster

> *'My drug use? You're joking! I thought this was about what my son has been up to.'*
>
> – Parent

Few parents explain to their youngsters just what they themselves got up to when they were young. Perhaps we are worried they will make the same mistakes as we did, that we will put ideas into their heads or that it will sound as though we are saying they can do the same.

Despite this, it is a good idea to let them know that we were young once. They might even learn something useful from our experiences – both good and bad. Try talking to your youngster about your drug use when you were young and your drug use now. Ask them what they think of it and whether they feel the same as you did when you were young.

Before you start this you might want to ask yourself some questions:

- What sort of an example does your drug use set for your youngster today?
- What are the good sides and bad sides of it?
- Are there ways in which you could improve?

> *'You know that I tried LSD when I was young.'*   – Parent

> *'I thought so. Look how you've turned out. I wouldn't touch the stuff myself.'*
>
> – 16-year-old

3: Be clear about your own attitudes to drug use

> *'We are all anti-drugs, aren't we? Now you tell me that we all use drugs, don't we? I get confused.'*
>
> – Parent

Many things influence attitudes towards drug use. These can include our experiences of drug use when we were young, stories in the media, our level of knowledge and our own insecurities. Most parents are against drug use when it involves young people and even more so when it involves their own youngsters. Some people go further and say that if we do not 'condemn' drug use then we must be 'condoning' it. Unfortunately it is not that simple. Nearly everyone uses some sort of drug. We tend to accept our own drug use as normal but criticise other people for theirs.

Also, our attitudes tend to change over time. We may have different attitudes towards drug use from our parents and they may be different from those of parents of friends of our youngsters. Our attitudes to drug use are also likely to be different to those of our own youngsters. Drug use is a very complex issue. So what are you supposed to think? A good place to start is to recognise where you stand and why. And be prepared for other people to have different views.

> *'Why should our attitudes to drugs be the same as our parents'? Their experience was totally different. The drugs around today just weren't available to them.'*
>
> – 16-year-old

Try this exercise. It might help you to think more about your own attitudes.

ACCEPTABLE OR UNACCEPTABLE?

Look at each of the situations below. Give each one a score out of a maximum of 10. Keep a record of your score.

0	1	2	3	4	5	6	7	8	9	10

Totally unacceptable   Totally acceptable

←   →

1. A seven-year-old has a small glass of wine with the family over Sunday lunch.
2. A 17-year-old smokes cannabis at a friend's house.
3. A 14-year-old inhales an aerosol in the park with some friends.

4. A 15-year-old comes home drunk after going to a Christmas disco.
5. A 16-year-old picks some magic mushrooms with some friends and eats them.
6. A 17-year-old takes half a tablet of ecstasy in a night-club and dances with friends till the early hours.
7. A 15-year-old smokes 10 cigarettes a day.
8. A 17-year-old injects heroin on a regular basis with their partner.
9. A 15-year-old is prescribed tranquillisers by the doctor because they have become very anxious.
10. A 16-year-old drinks at least 10 cups of coffee a day.

How many did you score on each question? Why did you score differently on different questions? Discuss the attitude quiz with your partner, a friend or another parent and see what they think of your answers. Even better, try it with your youngster and see whether they share your ideas. Remember it is likely that there will be different views.

Now have a look through the following list. How might each of these things influence your attitudes towards drug use?

- your own experiences of drug use
- the drug concerned (i.e. drug X is OK but drug Y is not)
- whether it is legal or illegal to use the drug
- the age of the young person
- whether they are male or female
- who they are with
- where they are and what they are doing at the same time as they are using drugs (e.g. at home, at a club dancing or driving a car)
- where you get your information from

How do the above influence your attitudes towards drug use? What other factors influence your attitudes? What factors might influence your youngster's attitude? The next section may help you to talk about it with them.

4: Talk and listen to your youngster

'My daughter wouldn't talk to me about it. But when I stopped and thought about it, I didn't really give her much chance.'

— Parent

Communication between parents and their youngsters sometimes breaks down when the youngsters are in their teens. There is often very little discussion and what discussion there is can end up as a shouting match. When it comes to drugs in particular, a lot of parents are very anxious talking to their youngsters.

Many young people also find drug use a difficult subject to talk about with their parents. What if the parents find out that they are using drugs? What if they cannot agree? It is not surprising that a lot of parents and youngsters decide to avoid talking about drug use at all.

When parents do get round to talking about drug use with their youngsters the danger is that they will do all the talking themselves. Quite often it will end up with something like, 'You wouldn't get involved in drugs, would you?'

As well as talking to your youngster you need to listen carefully to what they have to say. Try to do it in such a way that they feel they can tell you what they are really thinking and feeling (this section will give you some help on how to achieve this). Be aware that they might also know a lot more about drugs than you do and be able to teach you more about it. You can learn a lot from them.

'My parents were happy to talk about drugs. The problem was they never stopped talking. They weren't so keen on listening to me. Every time I said something they didn't like they just hit the roof.'

— 16-year-old

Try to leave them with the clear understanding that they can talk to you about drugs both now and in the future. Try not to make discussion of drugs a big deal but an everyday matter where different views can be tolerated and exchanged.

'My advice is, don't wait till a crisis to talk about drugs. Also don't make a big thing about it. Make it so it's a normal thing to talk about.'

– Parent

'If you make a big deal about it they just clam up and it goes underground. I'd rather know what they do even if it means I sometimes have to bite my tongue.'

– Parent

Blocks to talking and listening

Some things that get in the way of effective talking and listening are:

Ordering	'You must!' 'You have to!' 'You will!' 'You won't!'
Always advising	'What you should do is. . .'
Put downs	'You look stupid.' 'Other people will think you . . .'
Threats	'If you don't stop I will . . .' 'Wait till your father comes home!'
Lecturing	'Sit there and listen to me!'
Diagnosing	'What's wrong with you is . . .'
Undermining	'You are nothing but a no good . . .!' 'You're just stupid!'
Moralising	'If you had any decency at all you would . . .'
Interrogating	'Why?' 'Who?' 'When?' 'How?' 'Come on, tell me, admit it!'
Questions with-out an answer	'You wouldn't, would you?' 'I suppose you think drugs are OK, don't you?
Predicting	'If you do that . . . X will happen.' 'You will look silly!' 'If you carry on like this, you will . . .'
Patronising	'There, there. I'm sure it will be all right.'

Can you hear yourself speaking? Which ones do you use? What other things do you say or do to block effective communication? How could you improve?

Communicating effectively

Communicating effectively about drug use with your youngsters means:

1. Listening carefully to what they have to say.
2. Being flexible, agreeing to differ and being able to compromise.
3. Taking their ideas and feelings seriously.
4. Being realistic about their drug use and behaviour. Fashions do change, as do views on what is or is not acceptable.
5. Not putting them down or always criticising them.
6. Not going over the top, shouting or overreacting.
7. Not being too hypocritical. (Consider your own drug use both now and when you were young.)
8. Not making out you know things if you really don't know much.
9. Helping them reach their own decisions rather than always telling them what to do and think.
10. Being honest about how you feel and why.

These are difficult to do well and we all have room for improvement.

Try this exercise with your youngster.

TALKING AND LISTENING
– HOW GOOD ARE YOU?

1. Look through the list above together and for each item score yourself somewhere between 0 and 10, 0 being 'I'm hopeless at it' and 10 'I'm brilliant at it.'
2. Next ask your youngster what score they would give you for each item.
3. Discuss how your scores compare with the scores your youngster gives you. Also discuss how you could improve on each one.
4. Watch how you talk to each other over the next few weeks and see if you can both make some improvements.

Don't expect too much of yourself. Remember that we are only human. Being a parent is difficult and often lonely. We all have room for improvement and of course the perfect parent does not exist.

5: Put yourself in their shoes. What is it like to have you as a parent?

'It's tough being a parent. There is no proper training for it even though it's probably one of the most difficult jobs going. There is no such thing as the 'perfect parent', despite what they show in the glossy magazines. In the real world you just have to do your best.'

– Parent

Being a teenager, youngster, adolescent – even the words feel a bit awkward – is difficult. Being a parent can also be difficult. Being the parent of an adolescent is even harder. In today's ever-changing, high-pressure world, it is probably more difficult to be a parent than it has ever been before.

'They can't really win, can they? We expect them to be grown up but there is so much pressure on them these days – from us, their teacher, their mates. They probably feel everyone is watching them and passing judgement on them all the time and I suppose they are right.'

– Parent

Adolescence is an in-between world. It is like sitting on a fence but not being allowed in the attractive-looking gardens on either side. You are not a child any more and not expected or allowed to act like one. You have to be grown up and sensible, but you are not allowed to be too grown up and sensible. You are not given the same rights, freedom, independence and responsibilities as adults. Adolescence is about transition and change – physical, emotional, economic and social. But it is also about being in 'no man's land'. It is about experimentation and discovery, finding out what sort of person you are and what sort of person you want to be.

This can be very exciting but also very scary and full of contradictions. There are contradictions between the need for independence and feelings of insecurity, between wanting to make your own decisions and yet feeling controlled by others, between doing your own thing and yet being constantly criticised.

'What is it like being my age? Horrid. Now will you close my door on your way out?'

– 13-year-old

Some of the things adolescents need are:

- a chance to experiment
- to be trusted
- to be accepted for themselves
- to do adult things
- security
- space of their own
- for people to take an interest
- to have friends
- praise
- to make their own decisions
- understanding
- independence
- to choose their own friends
- to feel useful
- appropriate affection
- for it to be OK to fail
- reasonable rules and limits
- to be fashionable on their own terms
- to test boundaries
- not to be embarrassed
- flexibility
- to fit in with a crowd
- responsibility
- not to be made to feel awkward
- their own privacy
- to be successful
- not to be always criticised
- to be taken seriously
- help and advice when asked for
- consistency
- to be listened to
- to try out new things
- to make mistakes sometimes

Thinking about adolescence

Have a look at the list of adolescent needs and consider the following points.

1. Would you add anything else? If so, what?
2. Which were important to you when you were an adolescent?
3. Which ones do you think are most important to your youngster?
4. How do you help them with these things?
5. How do you hinder them with these things or make matters worse?
6. What could you do to help them more and hinder them less?
7. What do the things on the list have to do with drug use by young people?

Try talking through the questions with your partner, a friend, another parent and your youngster.

'We all have room for improvement. When you stop and look at yourself as a parent – if you can find the time – you realise that you can go a bit stale. But you can come up with new things to make it better. Not just for them, but for yourself as well.'

– Parent

'When you think about what being young and growing up involves I sometimes think it's a miracle that they are not all out of their heads on drugs all the time.'

– Parent

When I was young . . .

'Yes, I was young once, but it all seems such a long time ago. It seems like another person. You really have to stop and think hard to remember. I suppose my youngster is a bit of an angel compared to what I used to get up to.'

– Parent

What were you like as an adolescent? What did you find difficult? What did you find most difficult about your parents? In what ways is it different for today's youngsters? Why not tell your youngster what it was like for you and see what they think? Have the discussion with one of your own parents in the room if you can, three generations all talking about these issues together. What do you all think has changed for young people and what remains the same?

What about your needs as a parent?

You also have needs. You have a right to expect certain things from your youngsters. Some of the things we want from them are very similar to the things that they need from us. Have a look at the list of adolescent needs on page 82. Which of the things on the list do you want from them? What else do you want from them? Some other possibilities are:

- to know that they are OK
- to know what they get up to
- to know they think we are OK as parents
- to have them understand it's not easy being a parent
- to have them respect our views and values

Do you get the things you want from your youngster? If not, why not? Is it realistic to expect these things? If so, what could you do to make the situation better? In order to gain a better understanding of these issues, try the next exercise with your youngster.

―――――――――――― **LIKES/DISLIKES** ――――――――――

1. Parent: Write down two lists on a piece of paper. The lists should be of things you like about your youngster and things you find difficult about your youngster. Make sure that the first list has more things on it than the second one.
2. Youngster: Write down two lists on a piece of paper. The lists should be of things you like about your parent and things you find difficult about your parent. Make sure that the first list has more things on it than the second one.
3. The next step is to tell each other what you have put on your lists. Youngster, go first. Explain the things you find difficult about your parent. Parent, listen carefully to your youngster. Do not interrupt them all the time. Don't get into discussing each thing on the list.
4. Now, parent, it's your turn. Tell your youngster about the things that you find difficult about them. Youngster, you now

have to listen without interrupting all the time. Again, don't get into a discussion.

5. Youngster, now you tell your parent about the things you like about them.
6. Parent, now you tell your youngster about the things you like about them.
7. It's a good idea to have a quiet period now, just to think about what has been said.
8. Now discuss what has been said. In particular:
   a) How do you both feel about what has been said?
   b) What can you both do to improve your relationship?
   c) How this could help when it comes to drugs?
9. Try to work out some definite things you can both do to make improvements. Why not make dates for a few weeks' time to check to see what has happened?

You might also like to look at some of the other sections in this book together. The next section is about making sure your youngsters have a good drugs education.

6: Make sure they have a good drugs education

'I used to think it was best just to tell them to say no to drugs. I've learnt that it's not that simple. My youngsters went through a stage when they did anything that I told them not to. To me it's not just whether they use a drug or not – it's how they do it, whether they know what they're doing and what happens to them.'

– Parent

'My idea that they would never use any illegal drug was a bit stupid really. When you think about how widespread drug use is, especially cannabis use, there's more than a 50/50 chance in my area that your kid will be involved at some time or other. You can either face it sensibly or force it underground.'

– Parent

A lot of people think that if we educate young people about drugs they will not use them. The problem is that drugs education does not stop young people using drugs. Research into the impact of drugs education on young people has found that:

1. Trying to shock or scare them off drugs does not work.
2. Telling them not to do it can even encourage some young people to use drugs. This is especially the case if authority figures like police officers, teachers or parents forbid it.
3. Making a big thing of drug use is a mistake. It needs to be part of everyday discussion with young people.
4. All drugs should be considered, including alcohol, tobacco and medicines.
5. Drugs education should not be delivered as a 'one off'. It needs to be part of a full and ongoing programme of personal and social education.
6. Too often drugs information is distorted to make drug use seem worse than it is. Young people then find out from their own experience that it is not so bad. After this they will be very reluctant to trust adults again.
7. Trying to moderate drug use and to reduce the harm is probably more achievable than trying to stop all use of drugs. It is a question of having realistic aims.
8. There are no simple answers.

'Too many adults think that if young people are told not to use drugs or how awful it can be, then they won't use them. The problem is that most young people find out that it is not all bad. In fact many discover just the opposite – that drug use can be fun and brighten up their lives . . . and it's an even bigger buzz if your parents and teachers tell you not to.'

– Teacher

A good drugs education should give young people:

- Accurate and detailed information about the different drugs, their effects and risks. There should also be information on the workings of the law, the help that is available for drug users, etc.
- A chance to work out their own attitudes to drug use and hear other people's views.

- An opportunity to develop the ability to make their own informed choices about drugs.
- Chances to voice their own opinions, listen to others, argue and debate.
- The knowledge and skills to understand and help their friends and other people who might get into trouble with drugs.
- The ability to understand how complex the drugs issue is and the role of drugs in society.

Drugs education will not stop youngsters using drugs. However, it can make them better informed, more careful about what they do and encourage communication and openness about drug use. As a parent you can play an important role in making sure your youngster has a good drugs education.

Learn more together

1. Ask your youngster about the different places where they get their drug information.
2. Ask them about the drugs education they have had at school or college. What has it consisted of, what do they think of it and how does it match up to what we said about drugs education at the beginning of this section?
3. Ask them what they would like to find out more about. Add in your own thoughts and questions. What do you want to know more about?
4. Discuss how you could work together to find out more. (Some sources of further information are listed in Appendix II of this book.)
5. What about working through some of the sections in this book together?

Support sensible drugs education at your youngster's school or college

Many teachers are very nervous about drug education. They think parents will disapprove unless it consists of simple and hard-hitting anti-drugs messages. They probably know that these will not be effective, but they are sometimes not sure what other approaches they might use. Let them know that they have your support for accurate and sensible drug education that is designed to reduce the harms from drug use.

A lot of schools have recently come across drug use by

students. Some have panicked because they think parents will view their school as having a drug problem. Many youngsters have been expelled from school over drug incidents when there might have been better ways of handling the issue. (For further information about drug incidents in schools see page 112.)

So here is an action plan for you. You could:

1. Ask about what is going on at your youngster's school. Give your support to realistic and sensible approaches towards drug education.
2. Ask about how you might be able to help. This could include recommending that the school have a look at some of the resources we have listed in Appendix II. It might also include fund-raising for new educational resources. Many schools have very little money to buy new training packs, videos, etc.
3. Raise the issue through the school's Parent Teachers Association. Many schools have organised drugs awareness workshops for parents. Some have been led by drug experts and teachers but some have also had parents and students taking a leading role. Some PTAs have also raised money to buy the much-needed drug education teaching resources.
4. Raise the issue with the school governors. Do they have a policy on personal, social and health education (PSHE) that includes drugs? What does it say? Is it any good? Is it being put into practice? Does the school respond sensitively to actual incidents of drug use by pupils? What about elsewhere in the community?
5. Support other drugs education work for young people in your local community. This could include youth clubs and other youth and community organisations.

'It's silly really. We get more and more "Don't do drugs" and "Drugs kill" campaigns and at the same time more and more youngsters are using drugs. It's not the young people who need to think again. I think it's us. Clearly we have got it all wrong and need to be more honest and realistic.'

– Youth worker

7: Agree some drug rules with your youngster

'Agree, compromise . . . sometimes I don't think parents know what that means.'

– 18-year-old

Your youngster needs to know what you expect of them when it comes to drugs. It is no good not telling them what you expect and then going mad when they do something you do not approve of. You need to establish some drug rules. But you will not make much progress by just announcing them. You need to discuss the proposed rules with your youngster. Try to reach some sort of agreement. You need to negotiate with them. This means:

- listening to what they have to say
- being realistic
- being prepared to compromise
- agreeing to differ on some things

If the spotlight is going to be on their drug use it also makes sense to establish some rules about your own drug use at the same time. Your youngster is much more likely to follow the rules if they have had a hand in making them and the rules also apply to you. Try this exercise.

NEGOTIATING DRUG RULES

1. Think about your youngster and the drugs they might be using now or be likely to come across in the next few months. Which drugs are they? Cigarettes, tea/coffee, alcohol, glue, gas/aerosols, cannabis, amphetamines, LSD, ecstasy, poppers?
2. For each of the drugs you want to make rules about write down the following:
   a) What rules should apply to each drug? It could be not using the drug at all or, if it is to be tolerated, some idea of how much is allowed, when, where, with whom, how often, etc. Do be realistic about what young people do. There is no point in setting rules they cannot and will not keep to.

b) What should be the consequences of breaking the rules? You could include things like being grounded, fines, forgoing pleasant activities or taking on unpleasant activities.

3. Now ask your youngster to do the same exercise for your drug use. What do they think the rules, and consequences of breaking the rules, should be for your drug use?

4. Arrange a negotiation meeting. Have your ideas ready and ask them to have theirs ready.

5. First agree how you will run the meeting. Remember what we said about negotiation before. It is supposed to be a process of give and take, of compromise and careful listening. It should be fair. If you do not want your youngster to come home rolling drunk or to smoke cigarettes then should you?

6. Who is going to start, you or them? Take it in turns to explain the rules and consequences of breaking the rules you have arrived at. Don't get bogged down arguing over any one rule until you have both been through your ideas.

7. Now apply the negotiation rules and look for areas where you can agree. You may need to modify your ideas. You may need to trade rules.

8. Once you have reached some agreement, write down what has been decided about rules and consequences of breaking them. Both agree to try to keep to the rules.

9. Set a date and time to discuss the rules again soon. You will need to check how you are both doing and decide whether any rules need changing.

'I tried this exercise with my dad. It was great. I'm happy to hear what he thinks I should do, so long as I can tell him about his drinking and smoking.'

– 16-year-old

8: Anticipate how you would react if they were using drugs

'When we found out all we did was shout and argue. I argued with him about it. I fell out with my wife. If I'm honest, I caused more problems than his drug use ever did.'

— Parent

Part III of this book, 'Coping in a crisis', page 107, gives practical advice for handling suspected or actual drug use by your youngster. For now, try to think about how you might react. What if you were to find what looks like some drugs in your youngster's bedroom? What if they came in drunk or high? What if they were to tell you straight that they have used an illegal drug? What if they have been using drugs heavily for a time?

It can be very scary for parents to think about these types of situations. It is also difficult to predict how we would actually react. However, it can be useful to force ourselves to think about how we might react, how we should react and how we definitely should not react.

What would you do if . . . ?

Think about the situations below. If it was your youngster . . .

a) How would you feel?
b) What would you be thinking?
c) What would you actually do?

1. Your friend tells you that your 11-year-old has been seen smoking cigarettes on the bus on the way to school.
2. Your 14-year-old arrives home late one night drunk and smelling of booze.
3. You find a wrapper with a white/yellowish powder under your youngster's bed while you are emptying the bin from their room.
4. Your 16-year-old is brought home by the police after being caught smoking cannabis on a street corner.
5. Your 18-year-old regularly goes to clubs in the city centre. He returns the next morning and sleeps it off most of the next day.

Recently he has been very moody and lacking in energy. Last week the local paper had an article in it about 'Ecstasy and the club scene'. The way they described ecstasy users sounds just like your youngster.

6. You are all watching a television soap which has included a story about young people smoking cannabis and taking LSD. The parents in the soap are really angry with their youngsters about it. Your 15-year-old suddenly says, 'I don't know what the fuss is all about. Almost everyone I know uses cannabis.'

Now ...

1. Talk about the situations and your answers with your partner or a friend. What do they think of your reactions?
2. Talk about the situations with your youngster. How do they think a parent should react? What would they expect you to do in such situations? What do they think of your reactions to these case studies?
3. Draw up a list of DOs and DON'Ts for a parent responding to their youngster's rumoured or actual drug use. The DON'T list is quite easy, partly because it is always easy to say what we should not do.
   Some important DOs include:
   ● Listen to their side of the story.
   ● Make sure you do deal with issues that come up and not just hope they will go away.
   ● Tell them how you feel.
   ● Keep calm.
   Make your own list by thinking of situations you looked at before. (For more information on the DOs and DON'Ts of coping in a crisis see Part III of this book.)
4. Without being too hard on yourself, think about:
   a) which of the DOs you would find difficult
   b) which of the DON'Ts you would easily fall into
   c) how could you improve your reactions

'It's funny. I dreaded finding out she was using because you hear so many terrible stories. But it was a relief having it out in the open. It meant we could get on and deal with it. We still don't agree about it but I can see her point of view.'
                                                    – Parent

9: Learn basic first aid skills

What would you do if you found your youngster drunk, high, stoned or hallucinating? Would you know what to do? And what would you do if they had lost consciousness or stopped breathing? Do you know enough about basic first aid?

We are not trying to scare you, but we do suggest that you learn something about first aid. It is very unlikely that you will come across your youngster unconscious after taking drugs. However, it could happen and knowing what to do in an emergency can save lives.

If someone is heavily drunk, high or hallucinating and conscious . . .

- Don't try to talk about what has happened in any detail (wait till they have sobered up).
- Keep an eye on them and don't leave them alone.
- Sit them down in a quiet room. The half-sitting position is a good one (see diagram below).
- Open a window to let in fresh air.
- Talk quietly and calmly. Don't shout at them.
- Help calm them down if necessary. Reassure them.
- Loosen their clothing at the neck, chest and waist.
- If they are cold, cover them with a blanket but make sure they do not get too hot.

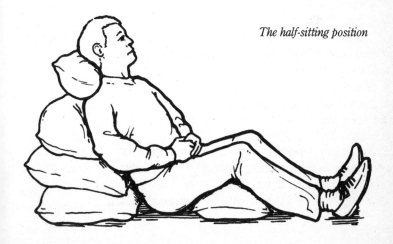

The half-sitting position

- Try not to give them anything to eat or drink. If they insist on a drink, give small sips of lukewarm water only.
- Do not move them unless it is essential.
- Do not try to induce vomiting.
- If you are still worried at all about their condition, keep them awake for a while before allowing them to sleep. Don't leave them to 'sleep it off' unattended. It can be difficult keeping people awake but it is very important. Each year some young people get very drunk, fall asleep and start vomiting. If unattended, this can be very dangerous, even fatal.
- Always err on the side of caution. Call a doctor or ambulance if you think it necessary.

If someone is overheating/dehydrated . . .

Drugs like ecstasy and amphetamine raise body temperature and give a boost of energy. If users take these drugs in hot places like clubs and dance for long periods they can lose a lot of body fluids. Overheating and dehydration can result. This can be very dangerous and has resulted in the death of over 70 young people in the UK since 1988. There is some evidence to show that this message has now got through to young people. Most of those using drugs and dancing know that they should 'chill out' and rehydrate by drinking extra water. Unfortunately drinking too much water can, in itself, be dangerous. Sipping a maximum of a pint of water an hour is now recommended for those using 'dance drugs'. Salt depletion can also be a problem for those drinking lots of water so it also a good idea to eat salty snacks whilst dancing and drinking water.

The warning signs include:

- feeling extremely hot and dehydrated
- cramps in legs, arms and back
- failure to sweat
- headaches and dizziness
- vomiting
- suddenly feeling very tired
- feeling like urinating but hardly being able to
- fainting or losing consciousness

It can be prevented by:

- Not dancing for long periods
- taking breaks between dancing

- sitting in cool areas
- wearing cool clothing
- not wearing caps or hats as they keep the heat in
- drinking water to replace fluids lost by sweating (no more than a pint of water for an hour of dancing – drinking too much water can itself be dangerous)
- eating snacks which contain salt and/or sodium
- avoiding alcohol and coffee (as they dehydrate even further)

If someone is overheating/dehydrating . . .

- recognise this by looking out for the symptoms above
- if the symptoms are present – call an ambulance
- move the person into a cool place (outside may be best)
- splash them with cold water and fan them to cool them

If someone has lost consciousness . . .

If someone has lost consciousness or you are having difficulty in waking him or her up, then call for help. It is better to have an unnecessary call out than a tragedy. If they are out cold, don't waste time with a doctor. Call an ambulance. In the meantime there are a few ways in which you can help:

- Clear the person's airway. Place one hand under their neck to support it. Put your other hand on their forehead and gently tilt their head backwards. Push their chin upwards (see diagram below).

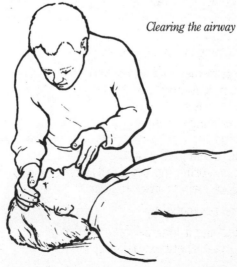

Clearing the airway

- Check to see whether they are breathing. Do this by checking if you can hear or feel their breaths. Put your ear against their nose and lips. Look to see if their chest or abdomen is moving.

If they are breathing. . .

- Loosen their clothing at the neck, chest and waist.
- Put them in the recovery position (see diagram on page 97).
- Stay with them and keep checking their breathing. Get someone else to ring an ambulance.
- If they come round, provide reassurance.

If they are not breathing. . .

Mouth-to-mouth resuscitation (the kiss of life) should be started straightaway (see diagram below).

- Clear their mouth of any dirt or vomit.
- Tilt their head back and lift their chin.
- Pinch their nose then take a deep breath. Seal your lips around their mouth and blow into it. Give them two slow, deep breaths. Their chest should rise as you blow in.
- Take your mouth away and watch their chest fall.

Mouth-to-mouth resuscitation

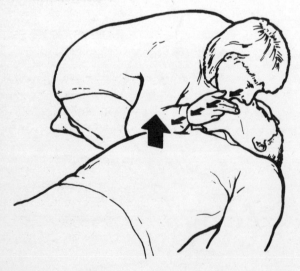

- Check their pulse to see whether their heart is beating. Do this by putting two fingers in the groove at the side of the Adam's apple and pressing firmly. If you can't feel a pulse within a few seconds their heart has stopped beating (see diagram below).

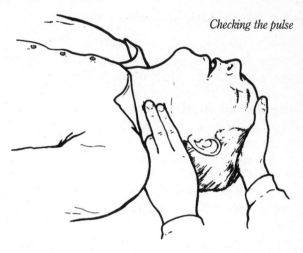

Checking the pulse

If their heart is beating . . .

- Continue mouth-to-mouth. Do 16–18 breaths in each minute (about one every 3 or 4 seconds) until breathing starts again or the ambulance arrives.
- When they start breathing again, put them into the recovery position (see below) and monitor their breathing.

The recovery position

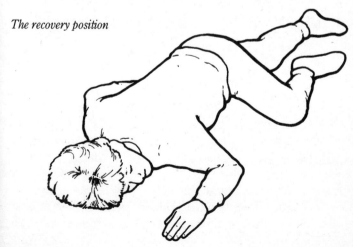

If their heart is not beating . . .

Heart resuscitation will be necessary. This is more complicated and we recommend that you look it up in a specialist first aid manual or learn it through a proper first aid training course.

If you want to learn more about first aid . . .

- A good book is *The First Aid Manual* published by Dorling Kindersley. This is the authorised manual for St John's Ambulance Brigade and the Red Cross. It is available in many bookshops or at your local library.
- Get some first aid training for yourself, your youngsters and other members of your family. Most areas of the UK have training courses provided by St John's Ambulance Brigade or the Red Cross or, in Scotland, St Andrew's Ambulance Association. Look up their numbers in your local phone book or ask at your local library, citizen's advice bureau, etc. (If you still can't track them down, the national office telephone numbers are St John 0171 251 0004; Red Cross 0171 235 5454; St Andrew's 0141 332 4031.)
- Ask your friends and your youngster's friends. Have any of them learned first aid? If so, could they teach you the basics? If not, would they like to find out more?
- Encourage first aid training for young people in your community. Every school should give all youngsters a basic course.

10: Know where and how to get help in your area

Don't underestimate what you can do to help. If your youngster needs help with a drug problem you may be the best person to help. Don't overestimate what professionals, experts and specialist drug agencies can do. They can help many users but they cannot succeed with those who do not want to make changes in their lives.

Users cannot be forced to accept help. They must want help themselves and not just any help will do. They need the types of help and people they feel comfortable with. If a young person does not want help there is no point in their parents trying to force them to see a specialist agency. Use of drugs by young people is sometimes not much of a problem for the young people themselves. Maybe it is the parent who needs the help – someone to talk through the issues with to help them understand their youngster's use of drugs and to decide how best to respond.

'It was silly thinking the people at the drug advice project would sort her out. I tried dragging her along but it was me who needed sorting out. They were really good in helping me sort myself out and then I worked it out with my daughter.'

– Parent

If your youngster does need help with a drug problem, start by thinking about help which might be closer to home. Who can help – what about family members, friends of the family or your youngster's friends? Don't rush off to the experts before thinking about other people whom your youngster may already know and trust. What about a teacher or a local youth worker if they get on well with the young person concerned? What about your family doctor? How would your youngster feel talking to them? Talk to your youngster about whom it might be best to approach for help and whom they would feel most comfortable with.

'The thing is, you think if it's drugs, you need an expert. If it's really heavy perhaps you do, but often young people prefer to talk to people they already know and get on with. He talked it out with the youth club worker round the corner. The youth worker talked to me too. She was good and it helped.'

– Parent

On the other hand, your youngster might need or want the help of a drug expert. The important point is to involve them as much as possible in the decisions. Try to help them to make it their own decision.

Find out what help is available in your area

You or your youngster might need some expert help on drugs in the future. Why not find out now what sorts of help are available in your area? The different types of help might include:

- GPs/family doctors
- Drug advice and counselling services
- Counselling services that specialise in working with young people around all issues, including drugs.
- Hospital based services.
- Residential rehabilitation.
- Self-help groups for drug users and for parents.
- Needle exchange projects for drug injectors.

More information about these different types of service is included in 'What kind of help is available?', page 59. If you want to find out what help is available in your area for people who have drug problems or want advice or information you can:

- Ask at your local citizen's advice bureau, doctor's surgery, library, council offices, social services, and school or youth community centre.
- Ring the National Drugs Helpline on 0800 776600. They should be able to tell you about services in your area.
- Ring SCODA (Standing Conference on Drug Abuse) on 0171 928 9500. They keep records of specialist drug services in each area of the country.
- Ring Release, who run a 24-hour national helpline specially for people who have been arrested for a drug offence. They also give legal and social advice to parents. They can be contacted on 0171 603 8654.
- And don't forget to ask your youngster. They may know about local drug services. They may also be able to help you find out more.

What should you find out about services?

Once you find out the name and address or phone number of the drug service in your area, don't feel shy about finding out more. Some questions to ask them include:

- What exactly do they offer?
- How can they help young people?
- How can they help parents?
- When are their opening hours?
- Can people refer themselves or do they have to go through a doctor or anyone else?
- Is it a drop-in service or do you need an appointment?

- If an appointment is necessary is there a waiting list and how long is it?
- Do they see people at an office base or do they do home visits?
- Is there any age limit? Will they see under-16s?
- Will they see youngsters without their parents being involved?
- What do they do about confidentiality, recording information and sharing it with other agencies?
- If your youngster goes in alone, do they tell you what happened?
- Are the staff members used to working with youngsters?
- Can you get any leaflets or other information about the project?
- Can they suggest any other local services that might help young people and parents about drugs?

SCODA, the national organisation for drug treatment services, has published a charter of rights and responsibilities for the users of drug services. It is reprinted below.

A drug service user has the right to :

- assessment of individual need (within a specified number of working days)
- access to specialist services (within a maximum waiting time) and the right of immediate access on release from prison
- full information about treatment options and informed involvement in making decisions concerning treatment
- an individual care plan and participation in the writing and reviewing of that care plan
- respect for privacy, dignity and confidentiality, and an explanation of any (exceptional) circumstances in which information will be divulged to others
- referral for a second opinion, in consultation with a GP, when referred to a consultant
- a written statement of the drug service user's rights
- the development of service user agreements, specifying clearly the type of service to be delivered and the expected quality standards
- the development of advocacy
- an effective complaints system
- information about self-help groups and drug user advocacy groups.

A drug service user's responsibilities to the service provider include:

- observing 'house' rules and behavioural rules, as defined by the drug service (e.g. not using drugs on the premises, treating staff with dignity and respect, and observing equal opportunities and no smoking policies)
- specific responsibilities within the framework of a care plan or treatment contract (e.g. keeping appointment times and observing medication regimes)

'We are more experienced at working with older drug users who are often injectors. We need the younger ones and parents to tell us more about what they want and how we can help them. I wish they would tell us more. After all, we are here to help them.'

           – Drug project worker

If you think your youngster needs or wants to use helping drug services

- Involve the young person as much as possible in the decisions.
- Make sure they understand what is on offer.
- Make sure they know how the service operates on things like confidentiality.
- Try to get them to think about what they want from the service.
- Encourage them to do the talking.
- Talk about how you can best support them – should you go along, should you go along together, etc.?
- If they are seen on their own, don't nag them to tell you what happened.
- If they are seen on their own, don't expect the staff to tell you what they talked about with your youngster.
- Don't expect any rapid changes.

'I was too shy to ask for help even though things were really bad and we needed it. I kept thinking about what people would think of us – we like to think we're a good family. Well, I soon discovered that we are pretty average like most families. My advice to other parents is if you really need information, advice or help grab it and don't hang around.'

           – Parent

11: Become active in your local community

'We don't ask enough questions – the really difficult questions like what is being done about drug use, why, what effect will it have, both good and bad, is it a good use of money? After all, when you think of it – police, schools, health, councils, MPs – there's a lot of hot air and it's our money that they're spending.'

– Parent

The drug issue is very complex and affects everyone in some way or other. What may be fun and pleasurable for one group of people can be a great source of anxiety and cause problems for others. Some users are damaging themselves and cause problems in their communities. Some users want to stop or moderate their use and can be helped to do so within the community.

Some users are involved in theft and burglary to fund their use of drugs. Some drugs, especially alcohol, will be implicated in violent behaviour, including male violence towards women and children. In some areas drug dealing has resulted in open gang warfare. In others, groups of youngsters using drugs on the street are seen as the main problem. In yet other areas, drug use mostly takes place behind closed doors.

No wonder drugs are such an emotive and complex issue. This makes it so important to think carefully and try to develop realistic ways of cutting down on the problems. Too often in the past people have oversimplified the issue and tried to find solutions which have either been completely unsuccessful or may even have caused new problems.

For example, telling schools to get tough on drugs has resulted in more schools suspending or expelling youngsters for drug use. This confirms the youngster as an outcast, may create anti-heroes and will certainly not eliminate drug use, although it may be forced underground.

Sending a heavy police presence into an area can disrupt drug supplies but may just move them into other areas. When the supply of one drug is restricted some users may move on to other, perhaps even more dangerous drugs.

In some areas there have been local 'anti-drugs vigilante groups'. The effects of such groups are rarely as intended. They may merely push drug use underground or move it on to neighbouring areas, making it more difficult to deal with problems when they arise. They can also result in a vicious circle of escalating violence. Whilst such efforts are understandable, they are not generally helpful.

But this is not a counsel of gloom. Whilst there are no simple 'solutions' to the drugs problem there are ways that you can help your local community to cope better with drugs. We have already mentioned ways you might work with schools, colleges and youth projects (see 'Make sure they have a good drugs education', page 85). Some other things you might do are:

1. Find out what local organisations are doing about the drug issue. You could ask local specialist drug services, health service units, the local council, the police, MPs, etc. and tell them your views.
2. Talk to other parents and young people in your area and see what they think. Have they got enough information? Could you get some leaflets for them or arrange for a discussion or talk?
3. Find out about local services (see 'Know where and how to get help in your area', page 98) and help campaign to improve services for young people – especially education and helping or counselling services.
4. Volunteer to help with local drug projects. It could be fundraising, decorating, counselling etc.
5. Start up a parent education or support group.
6. Talk to other people and help educate them.
7. Help develop good local leisure, youth and education facilities for young people. Lobby your local council to improve facilities.

Drug myths quiz answers

From page 70

1. *False*. We don't think a couple of drinks are usually dangerous. The same can be said about other drugs. It depends on what is taken, how much, the mood of the person and what they are doing at the time. (See 'What effects do drugs have and what are the dangers?', page 34, for more on drug risks.)
2. *False*. Use of alcohol and tobacco can be dangerous. These legal drugs claim over one hundred thousand lives each year in the UK.
3. *True*. Twenty to thirty thousand people die each year in the UK from the effects of alcohol. The comparable figure for all illegal drugs is about one thousand deaths a year. There are about 110,000 premature deaths a year from the effects of tobacco. The figure for solvents (glue/gas, etc.) has been between sixty and one hundred and fifty deaths a year for the last ten years or so. There are almost no recorded deaths attributable to cannabis use, although it can increase the risk of accidents whilst under the influence. There has been rising concern recently about motor accidents whilst under the influence of drugs.
4. *False*. Over 4 million people in the UK have tried cannabis and the overwhelming majority of these has never used heroin. There is no inevitable step from one drug to another. There is some research to suggest that those who start smoking tobacco at an early age are more likely to progress to other drugs than those who do not.
5. *True*. Only a small percentage of people who use drugs come to serious harm. Most users enjoy their drug use. Some users try it and decide it is not for them. We hear most in the media about the extreme cases where drug users come to grief. This is not to say that it is OK to use illegal drugs, but it is important to be honest about drug effects and not to exaggerate the consequences. Exaggerating the risks causes mistrust between adults and young people when they discover that many of their friends are using drugs, enjoying the experience and coming to no harm. We run the risk of losing credibility and becoming like the boy who cried wolf. When the wolf did come, no one was listening any more. We should try our best to tell the truth, the whole truth and nothing but the truth about difficult issues like drugs.
6. *False*. Users don't get hooked straightaway. Dependence, if it does develop, takes time. It can also vary a lot from person to person depending on their personality and situation. (See 'Why do young people use drugs?', page 21.) Most people who become dependent on drugs succeed in quitting in time.
7. *False*. Many of the heaviest users of drugs will commit crimes to finance their habits, but most drug users do not.

8. *False*. Not all youngsters try illegal drugs but the numbers of those who do is going up. In many areas there are now a majority of 16-year-olds who have tried a drug other than the legal ones – at least once.

9. *True*. Some leaflets list signs and symptoms of drug use but most of the symptoms listed are examples of normal behaviour such as being moody or tired. Symptoms like these can be due to many reasons other than drug use. Unless a youngster is under the influence at the time you will probably see no clear signs of drug use. (See 'How can you tell if your youngster is using drugs?', page 52, for more discussion on the signs and symptoms of drug use.)

10. *True*. The idea of the evil drug dealer who pushes drugs at unsuspecting young people is a bit of a myth. In most cases drugs are 'pulled' rather than 'pushed'. In other words, young people actively go looking for them or ask their drug-using friends for some. Drug dealers do exist but most youngsters get drugs from friends and acquaintances. (See 'Where do young people get drugs from?', page 25.)

11. *False*. It's true that most cocaine, heroin and cannabis is imported from abroad but cannabis is also grown in the UK. Drugs like amphetamine, LSD and ecstasy are often manufactured here as well as elsewhere in the world.

12. *True*. Illegal drugs are not always that expensive when compared to alcohol. This is especially the case for drugs like cannabis and LSD. Prices can be as low as a few pounds for a dose of LSD.

13. *False*. Who are the 'wrong sorts' of youngsters? We never think that our youngsters or we ourselves are the wrong sort. Illegal drug use is now to be found in every sector of society, every social class, both sexes and every ethnic group. The search for a scapegoat to blame for the spread of drug use amongst young people is a waste of time.

14. *True (probably)*. It is a safe bet that you use some drugs, perhaps caffeine (in tea, coffee, soft drinks and some chocolate), medical drugs, tobacco or alcohol. Yet most people tend to think of other people as drug users rather than themselves.

15. *False*. One problem is that most drug use is not that dangerous. Telling young people it is very risky can lead them to think we are lying to them or don't know what we are talking about. Their own experience and what friends say may tell a very different story. Knowing the facts is important to help people make informed decisions and know exactly what they are doing. There is research evidence to show that trying to shock or scare young people off drugs does not work and can sometimes be counterproductive.

How did you do? If you got fewer than eight right you might want to have a look back at Part I.

Part III
COPING IN A CRISIS

What can you do?

'What can I do? I must do something, but what? How could they do that? What did I do wrong that they want to do drugs? Oh my God . . . what if . . . ?'

Faced with a youngster using drugs many parents react with fear, anger or guilt – sometimes all three. One after the other, the questions swirl around, building up the pressure. The real enemy in this situation is the urge to do something drastic – anything – that will make the problem go away. Frustration and a sense of powerlessness can turn into anger and guilt and may lead to over-reaction.

So what can you do? The first thing is to recognise that all these feelings are normal reactions in such stressful situations. Here is a list of some common reactions and feelings on learning of drug use by a daughter or son:

- panic
- fearing the worst – maybe exaggerating the dangers
- getting very angry – going 'over the top'
- thinking something drastic has to be done straightaway
- trying to ignore it or pretend it hasn't happened
- arguing with partners or other family members over it
- blaming it on yourself and feeling guilty
- blaming it on other youngsters, drug dealers etc.
- trying to keep it a secret
- feeling very alone – thinking there is no one else who's ever experienced it before
- thinking there is no one who understands or can help
- thinking a drug 'expert' can sort it all out

Try not to give in to the fear or anger. Instead, give yourself time to think. Try to keep calm. Create some space and time for yourself. What is it that really demands an instant response? If there is a youngster flat out on the floor, then swift action is certainly needed (see 'Learn basic first aid skills', page 93). But most other situations can wait a bit whilst you get your own thoughts sorted out.

Get some support for yourself. You don't have to tackle these problems on your own. Is there another family member or close friend with whom you can talk things through? Be careful to pick out the most level-headed person you know. The last thing you need at this stage is being wound up by someone even more scared of the situation than you are.

If you don't have a friend or relative who would be calm enough to help you, there may be a local doctor or teacher or maybe a youth worker who might be able to help. There are a wide range of other people who might be able to help you through the crisis. Have a look at 'Know where and how to get help in your area', page 98, for advice on getting professional help.

Create some space for listening carefully to what your youngster has to say. This is explored in more detail below and in Part II of this book. The rest of this section tackles the sort of crises which parents often worry most about.

'It was a real crisis, but we all worked at it and pulled together. In time it got better, in fact we all got on better than we had before.'
— Parent

What can you do if you suspect that your youngster may be using drugs?

'I thought something was up but I kept saying to myself that I was imagining things. I left it for far too long before saying something and then when I did, it came out all wrong. I was really worried about them but it just came out like a big attack on them. That is not how I should have handled it.'
— Parent

The first principles are to keep calm and check your facts. Who says that your youngster is taking drugs? Are you sure? Have a look at 'How can you tell if your youngster is using drugs?', page 52. Remember it is important to communicate with your youngster, rather than just trying to spot the 'hidden signs and symptoms'. Likewise, if you have found a suspicious substance or object, look at 'What do different drugs look like?', page 49, and take care not to jump to the wrong conclusion.

You will also need to inform yourself about drugs and their use. If you rush straight off to tell your youngster about the horrors of drug use you could find yourself in the uncomfortable situation of realising that they know more about it than you do. You might like to read through Part I and Appendix I of this book to get some information first.

You will then need to talk to your youngster. Part II contains lots of ideas on how to talk to young people so that they listen and how you can listen so that they talk. If you suspect they are using drugs, do not jump in heavy-handedly and accuse them outright. Saying 'You're using drugs, aren't you?' is not a good starting-point.

> '*When they found out they just thought the worst. They accused me of all sorts I hadn't done. I understand they don't like what I did, but they could have listened to me.*'
>
> *— 17-year-old*

Equally, don't go to the other extreme and try to pretend you are not worried. Tell them what you are concerned about and why. Show that you are concerned about their welfare and that you care about them. Try to keep calm and be prepared to listen to what they have to say. Be prepared to be wrong in your suspicions. Also realise that even if they are using drugs they may find it difficult to tell you straight away.

> '*My advice to parents if they suspect but aren't sure is don't jump in with both feet. Think about it first. Talk it through with someone else first. Think carefully about exactly what you are going to say and carefully choose when to do it. Don't let it get out of hand. Overreacting just does not work.*'
>
> *— Parent*

What can you do if your youngster comes home stoned, high or drunk?

Keep calm is the first advice. If you do feel angry, try to manage the way you react. Anger is a natural response, but it can make things worse. Try to deal at a practical level. Are they flat out or just woozy? If they are having difficulty staying awake, don't let them 'sleep it off'. They may be in danger of a potentially fatal overdose or choking on their vomit – even on alcohol. If they are agitated or disorientated, try to calm them down. If they literally pass out and you cannot rouse them, you must put them into the recovery position (see page 97) and call an ambulance. It is better to be safe than sorry. There are more practical hints on dealing with an intoxicated youngster in the first aid section, page 93.

Leave discussion about the rights and wrongs of the situation until the following day. You will be calmer and they will be sober. You will be wasting your time trying to have a rational discussion with someone who is stoned or drunk.

The day after is the time to discuss rules for living together (see 'Agree some drug rules with your youngster', page 89). You have the right not to have your home regularly disrupted by drunken or stoned behaviour. Fortunately, it is only a small minority of young people who will use frequently in this way. You will have to decide if occasionally being drunk or stoned is acceptable to you.

'He came in completely out of his head. We tried to talk it out with him there and then. It just became a shouting match and he didn't know what he was saying. It's best to leave it till they are sober. The trouble is you feel annoyed with them there and then and it's hard being caring towards them. You have to look after them though – to check out they are OK.'

– Parent

What can you do if your youngster is suspended or expelled from school for drug use?

'It can be really scary having the head teacher and school governors accusing your kid and almost accusing you of being a bad parent. She did take a bit of cannabis into school. That was wrong and I agree she should be punished for it. But the way they went about it was like a murder enquiry – way over the top. It didn't do any good for her, for the rest of the kids or for us as a family. She did wrong but she needed us to help her get through it and learn from it.'

– Parent

Each year hundreds of young people in the UK are suspended or expelled from school for activities involving drug use. If this happens to your youngster the first step is to try and find out what really happened. Don't assume that your youngster is in the wrong. Mistakes are made, and a surprising number of suspensions and expulsions are based on hearsay and other evidence that would be inadmissible in a court of law.

Try to discuss the issues calmly with your youngster. They will probably be frightened of your response and it will not help if you are angry and shout at them. Have a look at the section 'Talk and listen to your youngster', page 78, for advice on talking and listening about drugs. Also, if they have not already spoken with you, discuss the matter with the relevant school staff. Ask them what they think happened and about the evidence they have to back it up.

A suspension is one thing and your youngster may be back at school quickly. An expulsion – or permanent exclusion – is obviously more serious. When you have a clear idea of what has happened you can decide with your child if you want to accept an expulsion or whether to appeal. If you decide to appeal, the first step will be to make an appointment to see the head teacher or their deputy. It might be possible to persuade them to change their mind in favour of another, lesser punishment, even if your youngster has broken the rules.

Most suspensions or expulsions involve the possession or supply of illegal drugs at school, although some cases have been about involvement with drugs outside school and a few have been because a youngster has refused to tell tales on another (drug-using) schoolfriend. Supply is usually punished more severely than possession but some cases of supply have involved the 'supplier' being bullied by other students – for example, when the 'supplier' has been known to be able to obtain drugs.

Schools will rightly want to give out clear messages that illegal drug use is unacceptable, but to do this it is not necessary to expel every youngster who uses or supplies an illegal drug. If schools were to catch and expel every youngster who had ever used illegal drugs between the ages of 14 and 18, they would end up expelling a majority of their pupils! There is no automatic rule requiring schools to expel youngsters. It is a matter of local policy and policy can be changed.

Even if the school confirms an expulsion, you have the right of appeal. In the state sector this appeal will involve the Board of

Governors of the school and the Local Education Authority (LEA). The exact way the appeal will work will vary from area to area. Sometimes the young person involved and their parents will have to attend a meeting of the school governors to try to convince them not to go ahead with the expulsion. The LEA may have an advisory teacher with a special interest in drugs issues who might be able to help you and will also have officers whose job it is to deal with cases such as these.

You will have a difficult decision to make about a possible appeal. Even if you win the appeal – and the odds may be against you – do you want to subject your youngster and your family to the controversy surrounding such a case? The local media may pick the story up – 'School drug scandal' might seem a very attractive story to them. Sometimes it can seem easier to let the matter be dealt with quietly and quickly get your youngster into another school. However, if you do not want to do this or there are no suitable schools nearby, you should feel free to lodge an appeal.

When under-16s are expelled they still have a right to full-time education. Your LEA should help with arrangements for entry to another school, but no school has an automatic duty to accept any youngster. You may have to shop around. For over-16s there is no automatic right to education. The worst harm to your youngster could come from being outside the school system completely for a few weeks or even in some cases, months. You may have to knock on a lot of doors to get action quickly but it is important to re-integrate them as quickly as possible. If your youngster is expelled your support as a parent is crucial.

You might be able to get specialist advice on how to cope with this situation from your local drug agency but not all drug agencies are experienced in dealing with such cases. See 'Know where and how to get help in your area', page 98, for more information.

'It is important in these situations that parents support their youngsters. Schools have a tendency to go over the top about drugs. I have been involved in a number of situations, which have been like kangaroo courts, and the head teachers have not known what they are talking about. One kept confusing cannabis and cocaine and kept mixing up which youngsters were involved.'

– Drugs education worker

What can you do if your youngster is arrested for a drug offence?

N.B. Information about drug laws and penalties is given on pages 43–8.

Young people under the age of 17 are only supposed to be interviewed by the police in the presence of a parent or guardian. Over-17s are treated as adults and parental involvement is not necessary. The first you know about it might be the police coming to the door or telephoning to ask you to come to the police station. Parents in this situation are often torn between their loyalty to their youngster and their desire to co-operate with and support the police.

The first step is to keep calm and to try to find out what has actually happened. Ask your youngster for their version of what has happened rather than assuming the police have got everything 100 per cent correct. Ask to talk to them without a police officer being present.

The police may let your youngster go without charging them. They may issue a caution. This often happens these days for first offences involving small quantities of illegal drugs for personal use, especially with cannabis. A caution means the youngster is not prosecuted and the case does not go to court. It usually involves a telling off by a senior police officer. It does not count as a criminal conviction but it is recorded and will be taken into account if the young person is caught again.

If your youngster has been arrested by the police they have a right to see a solicitor. It is a very good idea to get a solicitor. You are not acting badly if you insist on having one present during any discussions with the police. You will probably be under great stress in such a situation and an experienced solicitor will know how best to advise you. If you don't have one already, the police will have a list of duty solicitors whose job it is to turn out in such cases.

If the arrest is the first indication of any involvement with drugs by your youngster, you will probably be quite shell-shocked and need some time to work out how to handle the situation. Try to give yourself that time. Don't be pressured into hasty decisions which both you and your youngster might regret later. Your first decision might not be the best one. Asking for some time to discuss it in private and using a solicitor helps to keep your options open.

At the police station your youngster will have been seen by the custody officer whose job it is to complete and keep up-to-date the custody record. This is an important document that will have on it the details of the arrest, the reasons for the arrest and why the person arrested has been detained. The starting time of detention is also recorded there. Sometimes the police will ask you to sign this record to say that you do not want a solicitor. The legal rights organisation Release advises those arrested never to sign away their rights to a solicitor.

An arrest will be a very stressful experience for both your youngster and for yourself. Try to support them and do what is best for them. Don't start having a go at them about what they have done. There will be plenty of time to discuss what has happened later. The most important thing straightaway is to deal with the legal situation.

> *'It can be very scary and intimidating having to go down to the police station. I suppose I felt it was me who had been caught rather than my son. I felt angry with him and guilty myself so I felt I couldn't ask things or really stick up for him. Thinking about it, we should have asked them more questions and taken more time about answering their questions. And solicitors? My advice is, if it is getting serious, get a solicitor quick.'*
>
> – Parent

What can you do if your youngster is using drugs and doesn't see any harm in it?

This can be very difficult to cope with. Despite your best efforts your youngster starts to use drugs. They enjoy it and if you tell them not to they ignore you. They think you know next to nothing about drugs and they may be right. It is hard work being a parent. It can be really stressful just having a young person growing up beside you in your home. They see the world through their eyes not yours, whatever you do or say. Sometimes even when they are completely wrong they have to learn for themselves and make their own mistakes. There is no way they are going to do something – or not do something – just on your say so.

It can be terribly frustrating to have to sit on the sidelines

whilst someone you love does something stupid or puts themselves at risk – deliberately, it seems. Yet, if we are honest,
weren't we just like that when we were younger? Even if we
weren't, it doesn't alter the fact that young people can be head-
strong. They are in such a hurry to consume the world and all its
pleasures that they often seem to have no time to take care of
themselves in the way we want them to.

So what can you do? Well, first find out more. Have a look
through the first part of this book for general reference and look
up the drugs they are using in Appendix I, 'Facts about drugs',
page 127. This will tell you more about the risks they might be
running. Then have a look at your own attitudes and maybe
your own use of drugs ('Think about your own use of drugs',
page 72, and 'Be clear about your own attitudes to drug use', page
75). Try to understand their situation – 'Put yourself in their
shoes. What is it like to have you as a parent?', page 81, might
help.

Then take your courage in your hands and ask them to
describe to you just what it is they are getting out of their drug
use. Use 'Talk and listen to your youngster', page 78, for ideas on
how to talk and listen to your youngster about drugs and 'Agree
some drug rules with your youngster', page 89, for an exercise on
setting rules about drug. Make it clear to them that you want to
try to understand it from their point of view.

You will need to set clear rules if the drugs are being used in
your home. For example, you could be liable under the Misuse of
Drugs Act if you permit or tolerate the smoking of cannabis in
your home. 'What does the law say?', page 42 will give you back-
ground information on the legal situation and the rule-setting
exercise on pages 89–90 can help to agree drug rules with your
youngster about use in the home.

Depending on the drugs your youngster is using and their
methods of use you might want to check out if they are using in
the least harmful way possible. This harm-reduction approach is
the one most often used by drug agency workers. They will work
with a client to identify the most serious risks and make sure that
the client knows how to avoid them.

With cannabis, for example, the risks include unsafe sex whilst
stoned and being caught by the police and getting a criminal
record. With heroin, injecting is the biggest risk, for sharing inject-

ing equipment exposes the injector to blood-borne diseases like hepatitis and the HIV virus which leads to AIDS. Appendix I provides harm-reduction advice for situations in which people continue to use drugs.

It should also be stressed again here that in most cases the use of illegal drugs would be recreational. By far the largest number of drug users today are those using drugs like cannabis, LSD and ecstasy on nights out, at parties, in clubs and so on. Most of these users will take good care of themselves and come to no lasting harm. This is not the same as accepting their behaviour, but it is facing up to the truth.

Finally, don't close the door on further discussion with your youngster even if you cannot see eye to eye with them straight away. Leave them with the understanding that you will always be ready to talk to them again. One of the big problems with drug use is that it can undermine communication between young people and their parents. Points of view are often different, but that doesn't mean that we cannot keep talking.

> *'You can't live their lives for them even if you'd like to. I don't like her using but at least I know she is and I know something about it now. We do talk about it and I understand why she does it. I'm not happy about it. I never will be, but at least I know she knows what she's doing.'*
> – Parent

What can you do if your youngster is using drugs heavily?

Heavy drug use could involve daily use or regular 'binge' use of any substance. It could well mean the user has become dependent (see page 28). Most young people who use drugs do not use in this heavy, dependent way. It is only minorities who become so-called 'addicts'. For a full discussion of different levels of drug use see 'Why do young people use drugs?', page 21, but it is important to say here that the motives for heavy dependent drug use will be different from other types of more controlled drug use.

Faced with heavy drug use by their youngsters, parents have tried many different ways of coping. Some have tried to supervise their youngster more closely in an attempt to stop them obtaining drugs completely or, at least, to moderate their use. This has involved locking them in rooms, trying to keep them in the house or following them wherever they go.

Other parents have tried to cut off drug supplies by involving the police or directly confronting dealers. Some have even gone out to buy drugs for their youngster in an attempt to limit their drug use and contact with dealers. This is a very dangerous activity that puts the parents at risk of conviction for supply of a controlled drug – an offence that can lead to a very lengthy term of imprisonment. Some parents have arranged for their youngster to move elsewhere in the hope that a new environment and new friends and situation will break the pattern of drug use.

Although some of these measures are not ones we would recommend, it would be wrong just to condemn these parents who were trying their best in very difficult circumstances. There is no single correct way of responding to heavy dependent drug use. Some strategies work in some situations with some drug users and others don't.

Dependent drug users often have underlying social or emotional problems from which the drug use may represent an attempted escape. Heavy drug use can also produce its own problems of physical and psychological dependency, legal difficulties and chaotic lifestyle. These become overlaid on top of the existing problems of the user and the resulting complex of problems can be very difficult to unravel.

If your youngster has such a complex pattern of drug use, underlying problems and chaotic lifestyle, you would be well advised to seek specialist help. Your family doctor may be able to help if you think they will be sympathetic. Also help can be arranged from community-based drug advice services. Details of these services, and how to use them are in 'What kind of help is available?', page 59, and 'Know where and how to get help in your area', page 98. You can also get details of local services from the National Drugs Helpline by ringing the 0800 77 66 00.

A drug advice agency or family doctor will be able to work with your youngster if they are willing to accept their help. They will also be able to support you. Unfortunately, if the user does not want help there is little that can be done for them. If the young person concerned is under 16 years of age the drug agency may be reluctant to get involved and advise you to contact a youth service or social services department instead. In any event drug agencies should be able to advise you and help you cope better with the situation.

If your youngster has become dependent on drugs it will take time for them to feel better about themselves again. You may also have to face up to possible underlying family conflict that may have contributed towards their problems. Parents should not feel guilty about this. It is not as though they directly 'cause' all their children's problems. Many parents also face difficulties in their own lives. As well as focusing on giving support to your youngster, be prepared to set some limits and boundaries and to seek out help for yourself.

'It is especially difficult for parents when their youngsters get into really heavy use. They tend to blame themselves, which does not help anyone. Sometimes they try to cover it up and end up colluding with their child. They often forget themselves and the help they need for themselves. There are no simple solutions and what is best in one situation may not be best in another.'

– Drug agency worker

What can you do if your youngster is violent on drugs or steals your money or possessions to buy drugs?

Both of these are thankfully rare although they do happen. Parents in this situation need help for themselves and their youngster. Understandably they struggle to cope with such awful behaviour. Parents are caught between their love for their youngster and their horror and anger at how they are being treated. It can seem like the ultimate betrayal.

It does not help to start making excuses for the young person in this situation. Violence, abusive behaviour and stealing from the family home are unacceptable. We all have the right not to be abused in such a way. Just because someone is using or even dependent on drugs does not excuse such behaviour. Whilst there are those who would say that heavy drug users or 'addicts' are not responsible for their actions, we do not take such a view.

It is important to understand the terrible dilemmas of parents caught up in this situation but too much kindness in the face of abuse can sometimes make things worse. Long-suffering parents putting up with awful behaviour from their youngsters are a poor role model for them. When the youngster hits the outside world and treats others in the way he or she has learned to treat their parents, they may end up in terrible trouble or even in prison. By trying to be too kind and by accepting behaviour that is really unacceptable, parents can be setting up their youngster for trouble later on.

In the short term, the key task is to create some space and time to take stock of what has happened. You may need someone to talk to and support you, just as your youngster also needs help. With a young person under 17 your local social services department may be able to give you advice. There are also specialist drug agency workers who may have worked with parents before in similar situations. See 'Know where and how to get help in your area', page 98, and Appendix II, 'Where to find out more', for information on getting help.

If you are able to arrange some help for your youngster, be aware that this will only work out if they see themselves as having a real problem and want to help themselves. At some stage it might even be necessary to exclude the young person from the family home. Most parents would resist doing this to the bitter end, but sometimes it may be the only option. Some parents have called in the police in such situations or, with under-17s, arranged with social services to have them taken into care.

'It was terrible. It needed drastic action and I needed some help as much as they did. I felt awful about myself and blamed myself. I felt it was all my fault and then I felt terribly guilty about getting them to leave. But it couldn't have gone on any longer. Looking back, it was the right thing to do.'

– Parent

Part IV
CONCLUSION

To conclude the book we wish to emphasise a number of key points. These are:

1. Keep drugs in perspective – try not to exaggerate, overreact or panic.
2. Be aware of your own values and beliefs about drugs. Think carefully about where you stand and why and appreciate that other people, including your youngster, may have different views.
3. Increase your knowledge and awareness of drugs, but don't underestimate what you already know.
4. Distinguish between fact and myth. You don't have to become a drugs expert, but don't fall for the many myths which commonly surround discussion of drug use.
5. Try to appreciate what life is like for your youngster and what drug use – legal or illegal – may mean to them.
6. Talk to your youngster about drugs and listen carefully to what they have to say. Don't make discussion of drugs a big thing, but make sure they know that you are prepared to listen to them now and in future.
7. Feel free to seek out specialist help and advice if you and/or your youngster need it.
8. Don't become isolated. Talk to other people, especially other parents, about the drugs issue.

We value your views about this book. If you have any comment you wish to relay to us or have other ideas about educating parents about drugs, write to us at the address given on page 10.

Appendix I

FACTS ABOUT DRUGS

Introduction

'I talk to a lot of parents about drugs. They nearly always underestimate what they know.'
– Drug project worker

Lots of parents think that they know nothing about drugs but discover that they actually know quite a lot. To help further, this part of the book is for reference. It contains information about the following drugs:

    alcohol
    amphetamine
    caffeine
    cannabis
    cocaine and crack
    ecstasy
    heroin (and other opioids)
    LSD
    magic mushrooms
    nitrites (poppers, liquid gold)
    solvents (glues, gases, aerosols, etc.)
    tobacco
    tranquillisers
    other drugs (GHB, ketamine, khat and 'over the counter'
        medicines)

For each drug we give information about what it is, what its street names are, how it might be used medically, how it is taken, the extent of its use and its effects and risks.

We have also included harm-reduction advice for people who continue to use drugs whatever we advise them to do. The best way to reduce the harm from drugs is, of course, not to use at all, but some people choose to carry on using drugs and it is important to be realistic about this. The harm-reducing advice will help keep users as safe as possible until they decide to stop. In some cases it could be life-saving advice.

If you need to know about the legal status of drugs, refer to 'What does the law say?', page 42. If you need even more information about the drugs themselves, refer to the books or organisations listed in Appendix II, 'Where to find out more', page 154.

ALCOHOL

What is it?

Alcohol is a liquid containing ethyl alcohol. It is made by the fermentation of fruits, vegetables or grains.

Street names

Booze, drink, bevvy; individual types: beer, lager, wine, spirits, etc.

Medical use

In the past alcohol was given to hospital patients to help with a good night's sleep. Alcohol wipes are used to clean the skin prior to injections.

How taken

Alcohol is normally swallowed as a drink.

Extent of use

Over 90 per cent of British adults drink alcohol at least on an occasional basis. There are many young regular users. By age 16 over 95 per cent of young people have had a drink and over a third are already regular drinkers. As many as two thirds of 16- to 17-year-olds will be sold alcohol illegally. There are over 170,000 licensed outlets for the sale of alcohol in the UK.

Effects

Alcohol is a sedative drug. It slows down body functioning. Small amounts make users more relaxed and less inhibited. More can lead to poor co-ordination and slurred speech, double vision and ultimately loss of consciousness. The effects begin within 5 to 10 minutes and last several hours. The exact responses vary depending on the user's mood and situation.

Risks

Accidents are more common, especially when driving, operating machinery, etc. Too much alcohol in one go can lead to fatal overdose or losing consciousness and choking on vomit. Alcohol is associated with violent behaviour. The lowering of inhibitions can make safe sex less likely. Alcohol can be dangerous when mixed with other drugs. Long-term heavy use can lead to physical dependence and tolerance such that more is needed to get the same effect. Withdrawal from heavy use can lead to trembling and anxiety. High levels of use can also lead to heart, liver, stomach and brain damage.

Reducing harm

If someone is determined to use alcohol they could:

1. Be aware of the strength of different drinks and keep track of the amount consumed.
2. Not drive or operate dangerous machinery whilst under the influence.
3. Take a limited amount of cash with them when they go out.
4. Not get into too much round buying.
5 Remember the need for safe sex and always carry condoms.
6. Use non- or low-alcohol drinks.
7. Agree limits with drinking partners.
8. Look out for friends when out drinking. At least one member of the party could stay sober.
9. Not take alcohol with other drugs, especially sedatives like tranquillisers, heroin and other opioids and drugs like amphetamine or ecstasy especially when dancing.

AMPHETAMINE

What is it?

Amphetamine is a synthetic drug that comes in a variety of forms. These include a white, grey or yellow powder, tablets and a liquid contained in a capsule. Street use of amphetamines is likely to be in powder form.

Street names

Amphet, speed, sulph, sulphate, uppers, wake ups, whites, whizz.

Medical use

Amphetamines were originally developed as medical drugs in the 1920s. They were widely prescribed in the 1950s and '60s to treat depression and are still sometimes given as slimming pills. They were also given to soldiers to combat battle fatigue. Their current medical use is for narcolepsy (a tendency to fall asleep) and hyperkinesia (hyperactivity) in children, where the drug Ritalin has been found to have the paradoxical effect of slowing down hyperactive youngsters.

How taken

Amphetamine can be snorted up the nose in powder form. As a powder, pills or capsules it can be taken by mouth sometimes mixed in a drink. Amphetamines are also occasionally smoked and sometimes prepared for injection.

Extent of use

It has been estimated that between 5 and 18 per cent of 16-year-olds have used amphetamines at least once.

Effects

This is an 'upper' or stimulant drug which increases breathing, pulse rate, energy and alertness. A single dose can last three to four hours. Higher or repeated doses can lead users to feel they have increased physical and mental capacities. Sometimes after using amphetamines the user may feel anxious and restless and experience panic or feelings of persecution. These feelings wear off once the user has stopped taking the drug.

Appetite tends to be suppressed and sleep delayed. This explains the use of amphetamines by slimmers and people who need to stay awake. Once the effect wears off users can be very tired, needing some time to recover.

Risks

The best known street name for amphetamine – speed – highlights its main effect. The fact that it is a bit like borrowed energy means that users will sometimes need time to recover after a long session of use. They may find it difficult to stick to a normal work routine. It can also result in users overdoing physical activity and possibly becoming too hot and dehydrated, e.g. from all-night dancing.

The strong stimulant effect can also be dangerous to people with heart or blood pressure problems. Long-term use of amphetamines can result in tolerance developing (i.e. more being taken to get the same effect) and lack of food and sleep. This can reduce the user's resistance to illness. Some regular users get very panicky and feel other people are getting at them.

Although physical dependence is not a problem, giving up long-term use can be very difficult, as users can feel depressed and lethargic when not using the drug. They may have come to rely on the lift that it gives them.

Reducing harm

If someone is determined to use amphetamine they could:

1. Try to maintain normal work, diet and sleep routines, as far as possible.
2. Use a limited amount of the drug on an occasional basis and take breaks from use.
3. Allow enough time to recover from each session and let the body recharge its batteries.
4. Not overdo strenuous physical activity whilst using the drug.
5. Take breaks and drink sufficient water to replace body fluids lost through sweating if engaged in physical activity such as dancing or running.
6. Drinking too much water can, in itself, be dangerous. Sipping a maximum of a pint of water an hour is now recommended for those using 'dance drugs'.
7. Salt depletion can also be a problem for those drinking lots of water so it also a good idea to eat salty snacks whilst dancing and drinking water.
8. Be given reassurance and 'talked down' if they become anxious.
9. Take care to use clean equipment if injecting amphetamine. Avoid sharing injecting equipment.
10. Not mix amphetamine with other drugs.

CAFFEINE

What is it?

Caffeine is a drug found in tea, coffee, cocoa, many soft drinks such as cola, some chocolate and some medical tablets.

Medical use

Caffeine has been used in various medical preparations, for example, to ease headaches and to ease passing of water.

How taken

Swallowed in a drink or eaten in confectionery or in pill form.

Extent of use

Most adults and many youngsters use caffeine on a daily basis.

Effects

Caffeine is an 'upper' or stimulant drug. It combats drowsiness and tiredness. It can also aid concentration. Its use increases heart rate and blood pressure. The effects start quickly and can last for a few hours. Using caffeine makes people urinate more. High doses can result in headaches and irritability.

Risks

Regular, high dosage users of caffeine usually become dependent. Those taking more than about six to eight cups of instant coffee or tea a day may well experience withdrawal symptoms if they try to give up the drug. Going without the drug can lead to symptoms such as feeling irritable, tiredness and headaches. Dependence on caffeine is usually socially acceptable. Heavy, long-term use may increase risk of peptic ulcers, kidney, bladder and heart disease and blood pressure problems.

Reducing harm

If someone is determined to use caffeine they could:

1. Try decaffeinated or lower strength tea and coffee products as well as herbal teas, etc.
2. Keep a record of the amount consumed and set daily limits.
3. Take a break from use on one or two days a week.

CANNABIS

What is it?

Cannabis comes from the *Cannabis sativa* plant that grows all over the world. Whilst most of it is imported into the UK there is also some home-grown cannabis. The leaves from the plant (known as grass, bush, weed, etc.) can be smoked or eaten, or the drug can be concentrated into a resin block or oil form. In recent years stronger forms of cannabis have become available in the UK.

Street names

Bhang, black, blast, blow, Bob Hope, bush, dope, draw, ganja, grass, hash, herb, marijuana, pot, puff, resin, rocky, rope, sensi, shit, skunk, sputnik, wacky backy, weed, zero zero (or double zero) and many other names. Some of the street names for cannabis are based on the country of origin, e.g. Afghan, Colombian, Lebanese, Moroccan, etc. A 'J', 'joint', 'reefer' or 'spliff' is a cannabis cigarette made with cigarette papers. A 'roach' is the filter that is often made of a rolled-up piece of card.

Medical use

There has been no official medical use in the UK although cannabis can be used in the treatment of glaucoma (a disease of the eye), arthritis, AIDS, multiple sclerosis (MS) and to relieve the side effects of chemotherapy used in cancer treatment. Recently a cannabis substitute was prescribed to help alleviate the effects of multiple sclerosis (MS). It is widely used as a folk remedy in various parts of the world and was commonly used in this way in Victorian Britain, including reportedly by Queen Victoria to relieve period pains.

How taken

Herbal cannabis can be smoked by itself or with tobacco in a cigarette or pipe. The resin can be smoked and is sometimes eaten. Both resin and herbal forms are also sometimes cooked into dishes. Cannabis oil is usually coated on cigarette papers and smoked with tobacco.

Extent of use

Cannabis is the most widely used illegal drug in the UK. It has been estimated that there may be 2 million regular users, with many more having used it in the past.

Effects

The effects of cannabis are often dependent on the user's moods and expectations. Users often report feeling more relaxed, giggly and talkative, with enhanced appreciation of sound and colour. It can also sometimes make users anxious and nervy, especially if they are uneasy to start with. Cannabis use affects concentration, thinking and manual skills. Feelings of hunger and forgetfulness are common. The effects start quickly and can last several hours.

Risks

There is no danger of fatal overdose or physical dependency. As with any drug, psychological dependence can develop. If the user becomes reliant on the drug to help with relaxation it can become difficult to do without. Long-term heavy smoking of cannabis may lead to lung disorders. There is also a risk of accidents whilst under the influence, especially whilst driving. Using cannabis can make practising safe sex more difficult as it tends to lower inhibitions. Taking high doses whilst feeling depressed or anxious can lead to paranoia.

Reducing harm

If someone is determined to use cannabis they could:

1. Avoid driving or operating dangerous machinery whilst under the influence.
2. Remember the need to practise safe sex – always carry condoms.
3. Take care where it is used. Over 75,000 people are prosecuted or cautioned each year in the UK for the illegal possession of cannabis.
4. Be given reassurance if feeling anxious or paranoid under the influence.
5. Have a few days off from using every week. This will prevent any psychological dependence creeping up unawares.
6. Not eat large lumps of cannabis. This can be very disorientating as too much can be taken in one go.
7. Avoid particularly strong types of cannabis.

COCAINE AND CRACK

What is it?

Cocaine is derived from the coca shrub from South America. It is first made into coca paste then refined to produce cocaine, which is usually a white crystalline powder. Crack, a form of cocaine that is smokable, is so-called 'freebase' cocaine and comes in small, crystalline lumps or 'rocks'.

Street names

Cocaine is known as C, Charlie, coke, dust, gold dust, lady, snow, white. A 'line' is a line of cocaine powder ready for sniffing. Crack is known as base, freebase, gravel, ice, rock and wash.

Medical use

Cocaine is rarely used in medicine today. In the past it was used as a local anaesthetic. Until 1904 Coca-Cola contained small quantities of extract of coca and was marketed as a tonic. Sigmund Freud, the renowned psychoanalyst, was once an enthusiastic user and advocate of cocaine.

How taken

Cocaine powder is usually sniffed up the nose, often through a rolled banknote or straw, but is sometimes made into a solution and injected. Crack is smoked in a pipe, glass tube, plastic bottle or on foil. The smoke from the heated rocks is inhaled.

Extent of use

Its use is patchy in the UK. Cocaine tends to be expensive and mainly used by the wealthy. Crack use has become more prevalent in major cities but is not widely used. Surveys usually show that only 1 per cent of 16-year-olds have tried cocaine or crack.

Effects

These are stimulant drugs that can make users feel alert, confident and strong. At higher dose levels they can also make users feel anxious and panicky. The effects come on strongly within 5–10 minutes but die away quickly. The dose needs repeating about every 20 minutes to maintain the effect.

Risks

Large doses can make users feel very anxious. The stimulant effect can be followed by feelings of depression and fatigue. Although cocaine is not a drug that normally results in physical dependence, users can be tempted into regular use in an attempt to maintain feelings of energy and power and avoid depression and 'lack of go'. This is particularly the case with crack that often has an especially intense high and can lead to cravings for more. Heavy, regular use can result in restlessness, nausea, insomnia and paranoia. Repeated sniffing of cocaine can damage the nasal passages. Repeated smoking of crack can lead to wheezing and loss of voice. Injecting cocaine carries risks of infection by blood-borne viruses such as HIV and hepatitis if injecting equipment is shared.

Reducing harm

If someone is determined to use cocaine or crack they could:

1. Try to avoid regular use.
2. Keep a record of the amounts taken and the costs involved and set limits.
3. Sniff cocaine rather than smoke crack.
4. Try to maintain regular sleep and diet patterns.
5. Allow recovery time from each session of use. Have a day or two off from use every week.
6. Avoid injecting if possible but otherwise take care not to share injecting equipment.
7. Not mix cocaine with other drugs (especially heroin and other depressants).

ECSTASY

What is it?

Ecstasy is an illegally manufactured drug in tablet or capsule form. The chemical name is MDMA -3,4 methylene-dioxymetham-phetamine. Other, similar, drugs such as MDA or MDEA are sometimes sold as ecstasy.

Street names

Adam, big brownies, burgers, California sunrise (also sometimes LSD), Dennis the Menace, disco biscuits, doves, E, Edward, essence, fantasy, love doves, M and Ms, MDMA, M25s, New Yorkers, rhubarb and custard, shamrocks, white doves, X, XTC and many others.

Medical use

It was originally manufactured in Germany in the early twentieth century as an appetite suppressant. There is no current medical use, although some doctors have suggested it could be used for those with long-term mental health problems and in couples' therapy.

How taken

Ecstasy is usually swallowed as tablets or capsules.

Extent of use

It has become very popular amongst young people since 1988.

There are recent estimates of up to 500,000 regular users in the UK.

Effects

This is a stimulant drug with mild hallucinatory properties. It tends to make users feel more energetic. Many users report calmness, loss of anger and hostility, empathy with others and an enhanced sense of communication. There can also be a heightened sense of surroundings and sound appreciation. Sometimes users can feel nausea and disorientation. Clenching of the jaw and loss of appetite is common. The effects start after 20–60 minutes and can last for several hours.

Risks

With high doses anxiety and confusion can result, especially if users are already panicky. Regular users can experience sleep problems, lack of energy and depression. Whilst physical dependency is not a problem, psychological dependency on the feelings of calmness and euphoria associated with the use of the drug can develop. Little is yet known about the physical effects of long-term heavy use.

There is an increased danger of accidents whilst under the influence. There is also a problem of identification. Ecstasy can be difficult to distinguish from other drugs. Users are sometimes unsure about what drugs they are taking and what effects it will have. LSD and amphetamine have both been sold as ecstasy. Other so-called 'E tablets' have been found to contain no ecstasy and a variety of other home-made drugs or adulterants (see also ketamine, below).

Safe sex may be more difficult under the influence, especially with ecstasy's 'love drug' image. There have been over 70 deaths associated with ecstasy use in the UK. Many have been connected with non-stop physical activity whilst under the influence leading to overheating and dehydration. Drinking alcohol increases the risk. Drinking water to replace fluids lost through sweating and taking a break from dancing ('Chillin' out') make overheating and dehydration less likely. However, drinking excessive amounts of water can, in itself, be dangerous as shown in the tragic and much publicised case of Leah Betts. For this reason a limit of one pint of water an hour is the recommended maximum. Salt depletion has also been recognised as a possible problem so those using 'dance drugs' are also advised to eat snacks containing salt or sodium.

Ecstasy use may also be particularly dangerous for people who have heart or blood pressure problems.

Reducing harm

If someone is determined to use ecstasy they could:

1. Avoid regular use i.e. not use every weekend.
2. Take care what is being used. Many tablets contain other drugs and adulterants.
3. If unsure about the strength of the drug, not take a full tablet. Some users see what happens with half a tablet or smaller amounts first rather than going straight to full or multiple tablets.
4. Avoid too much continuous strenuous physical activity such as dancing non-stop.
5. Take breaks from dancing and drink water to replace lost body fluids (not alcohol – it dehydrates even more). No more than a pint of water an hour is advised if people are dancing non-stop as too much water can itself be dangerous.
6. Eat some snacks containing salt or sodium to counter salt depletion from drinking lots of water.
7. Be reassured and talked down if they become disturbed.
8. Avoid driving or operating dangerous machinery whilst under the influence.
9. Not use with other drugs, especially alcohol.
10. Remember to practise safe sex and always carry condoms.

HEROIN (AND OTHER OPIOID DRUGS)

What is it?

Heroin is a powder derived from the opium poppy. There are also many other opioid (opiate-type) drugs that are manufactured from synthetic chemicals.

Other opioids

These include codeine, diconal, di-hydrocodeine (DF 118s), methadone, morphine, opium, palfium, pethidine and temgesic.

Street names

For heroin: boy, china white, dragon, gear, H, Harry, horse, jack, junk, scat, skag, smack.

The names for other opioids include dike, DFs, dollies, M, meths, morph, palf, phy' amps, etc.

Medical use

There is extensive medical use of opioids. Heroin and morphine are prescribed as strong pain relievers. Pethidine is often prescribed to women in childbirth. Other opioids are widely used for pain relief, as cough suppressants, anti-diarrhoea treatments, etc. Methadone is frequently prescribed as a treatment for heroin dependence. The aim is to supply a slow-acting heroin-like drug that does away with the need for the user to seek out street supplies of their drug. Occasionally heroin is itself prescribed for drug users, but these days this is very rare.

How taken

Heroin can be smoked, sniffed or injected. Most other opioids are taken orally in tablet or liquid form. Tablets can be crushed and made into a solution for injection.

Extent of use

Heroin is the most commonly used illicit opiate. The number of people using heroin on a regular basis in the UK has been estimated at over 100,000 but no one knows the exact figure. Other opioids are prescribed and sometimes used illegally. In surveys of teenagers usually less than 1 per cent claim to have used heroin even once. However, recent reports have suggested more use of heroin and methadone by young people in deprived areas and a fall in the price of heroin.

Effects

Opioids are sedative drugs. They slow down body functioning and give a feeling of warmth. Use is followed by feelings of relaxed detachment, removal of feelings of anxiety and blocking of feelings of physical and emotional pain. Higher doses can result in sedation and drowsiness. Effects start quickly and can last several hours, but this varies with how the drug is taken.

Risks

With regular use tolerance develops (more is needed to get the same effects) and physical dependence can result. Withdrawal after regular heavy use can produce unpleasant symptoms like a severe bout of 'flu, making it difficult to 'kick the habit'. Stopping dependent use for a short time is one thing. Staying off longer term can be much more difficult. Funding a heroin habit can be very expensive and unless users have a lot of money they may find that they have to steal regularly to get money. Getting into debt and violent situations may follow, as may getting a criminal record.

Large doses can result in coma and possibly death. It is difficult to know sometimes just how much is being taken, as street drugs like heroin are normally mixed with adulterants. The strength of dose will vary and the adulterants can themselves be dangerous. Injecting will make these more serious, as well as putting users at risk of blood-borne infections such as HIV and hepatitis if sharing injection equipment.

Reducing harm

If someone is determined to use heroin they could:

1. Avoid everyday use.
2. Be aware of the risks from variable strength and adulterants, especially if injecting.
3. Maintain a regular daily routine, sleep and diet patterns.
4. Smoke rather than inject the drug.
5. Not share injecting equipment. Use a needle exchange to get new syringes.
6. Have a clean break from use every few days. When returning to use later, remember that tolerance will have fallen off. Amounts previously taken safely could now lead to fatal overdose.
7. Not mix heroin with other drugs especially other depressants (including alcohol or tranquillisers).
8. Seek alternatives such as a prescription of oral methadone if available.

LSD

What is it?

This is an illegally manufactured drug called Lysergic Acid Diethylamide. Only very small quantities are needed to get an effect. It is usually made into impregnated paper squares, tablets or capsules.

Street names

A, acid, blotter, cheer, dots, drop, flash, Gorbachovs, hawk, L, lightning flash, Lucy, micro dot, paper mushrooms, penguins, rainbows, smilies, stars, strawberries, sugar, tab, tripper, trips, window and many other names.

Medical use

There is no current medical use for LSD. Previously there was some medical prescribing to long-term mentally ill patients but this was abandoned, as the effects were too unpredictable.

How taken

LSD is usually swallowed as a capsule, pill or impregnated paper square.

Extent of use

LSD was very popular in the 1960s' and '70s' 'hippie' culture. It has recently come back into fashion with younger users. It is often taken these days at parties and raves alongside amphetamine and/or ecstasy. In local surveys up to 24 per cent of 16-year-olds claim to have used LSD but it tends to be used on an occasional basis rather than regularly.

Effects

LSD is a hallucinogenic drug. A 'trip' begins about 30 minutes to an hour after taking it and can last up to 12 hours. The effects will vary depending on the person, their mood and the situation. There can be sight and sound distortions, the intensification of colours and changes in sense of time and place.

Some users report heightened awareness of themselves and other people and almost mystical experiences. Feelings of being outside the body are also common. Whilst an LSD trip can be exciting it can also sometimes be very frightening. A 'bad trip' can be very disturbing and include strong feelings of panic and being persecuted.

Risks

Unpleasant reactions can include anxiety, depression, paranoia and feelings of persecution and encroaching madness. This may be dangerous if users are already depressed or suicidal.

Accidents from driving or operating machinery are possible after using the drug, as it will make concentration on any task difficult. There is no evidence of physical dependency or any danger of fatal overdose. There is a built-in incentive not to use too often as after a few days of continuous use further doses are ineffective without a few days' break.

There is no known physical damage from even long-term use, although some users report 'flashbacks', i.e. re-experiencing a 'trip' some time afterwards. This can be disturbing, especially when the user does not know what it is.

Reducing harm

If someone is determined to use LSD they could:

1. Take care with the amount consumed. If unsure take a very small quantity and see what happens.
2. Avoid using LSD when feeling anxious or depressed.
3. Plan carefully in whose company it is used. Make sure that the situation is under control and comfortable before using.
4. Be talked down and reassured if they become disturbed.
5. Understand that whilst flashbacks can be scary, they don't mean that one is going mad. Flashbacks will go away after a while.

MAGIC MUSHROOMS

What are they?

They are hallucinogenic mushrooms that grow wild in many parts of the UK in autumn. The main type is liberty cap (*Psilocybe*) but fly agaric (*Amanita muscaria*) is also sometimes used.

Street names

Liberties, mushies, 'shrooms.

Medical use

None.

How taken

The mushrooms are eaten raw or sometimes after being dried out. They can also be cooked with and then eaten or made into a tea or infusion and drunk.

Extent of use

There is a lot of experimenting by young people every autumn. More liberty caps are used than fly agaric. Local surveys have shown 5–15 per cent of 16-year-olds claim to have tried them at least once.

Effects

This is a mild hallucinatory drug. Its effects vary depending on the person and their mood, the situation of use and the expectations of the users. Effects begin after about half an hour and can last up to nine hours, depending on how many are taken. Users often laugh a lot and report feeling more confident. Higher doses give a mild 'trip' with visual and sound distortions. Some people feel nausea and experience vomiting and stomach pains.

Risks

A bad 'trip' can be unpleasant and scary. The effects of such a trip can include nausea, vomiting and paranoia. There is an increased danger of accidents whilst under the influence. There is no evidence of physical dependence or physical harm from use. The fact that much more is needed to get the same effect from a repeat dose means users usually have a gap between using and do not use too often. One other real danger is taking the wrong type by mistake and being poisoned. The symptoms of food poisoning include nausea, stomach cramps, vomiting and diarrhoea. If this becomes severe, it is best to consult a doctor.

Reducing harm

If someone is determined to use magic mushrooms they could:

1. Be absolutely certain that they know what they are taking. Many wild mushrooms are poisonous.
2. Carefully control the number taken. Twenty liberty caps or three fly agarics will bring on effects in most cases.
3. Avoid fly agaric, whose effects are less predictable.
4. Avoid using any mushrooms if they are feeling anxious or depressed.
5. Carefully plan whom they use with, how and where. Try to choose a calm, friendly situation with friends around to support them if they should become panicky.
6. Be talked down and reassured if they become disturbed.

NITRITES (POPPERS, LIQUID GOLD)

What is it?

A gold-coloured liquid called amyl or butyl nitrite. It usually comes in a bottle or in small glass 'vials' containing the liquid, which are 'popped' open and the vapours inhaled (giving the street name 'poppers').

Street names

Amyl, liquid gold, locker room, poppers, ram, rock hard, rush, snapper, stag, stud, thrust, TNT.

Medical use

There is no current medical use. In the past nitrites from the same family were used for relief of angina/chest pains. They do this by dilating the blood vessels, allowing more blood to get to the heart.

How taken

Vapours from the liquid are inhaled through the nose and/or mouth.

Extent of use

Nitrites are widely available in clubs, from joke and sex shops and from some young people's clothes and record shops. This situation should have changed with the incorporation of some types of nitrites under the Medicines Act but in practice this has not happened (see page 47). At one time nitrites were most commonly used in gay clubs but in recent years nitrites have become much more popular with all young people. Local surveys show up to 23 per cent of 16-year-olds claiming to have used them at least once.

Effects

The effects start straightaway but only last a few minutes. The acceleration of heartbeat and rush of blood to the brain gives a 'rushing' feeling. Users often say they feel time is slowed down. Loss of balance is common and headaches and nausea can result. Users say that nitrites prolong orgasm and thus enhance sexual pleasure. It has also been claimed to prevent premature ejaculation in men.

Risks

Users can lose consciousness, especially if they are involved in vigorous physical activity like dancing or running. Accidents are more likely whilst under the influence. Use of nitrites could lead to a heart attack in people who have blood pressure or heart problems. This drug also increases pressure within the eyeball and should not be used by people who have glaucoma.

Regular use can lead to skin problems around the nose and lips. There are also reports of fatalities when users have drunk the liquid neat rather than inhaling the vapour. Some regular users have reported prolonged headaches.

Using nitrites can make safe sex more difficult to put into practice. Use does not lead to physical dependence and there is no definite evidence of long-term health damage.

Reducing harm

If someone is determined to use nitrites they could:

1. Never drink the liquid – only inhale the vapours.
2. Take care not to use when undertaking strenuous physical activity.
3. Not drive or operate machinery under the influence.
4. Avoid using if they have heart disease, blood pressure problems or glaucoma.
5. Remember to practise safe sex.

SOLVENTS (GLUE, GAS, AEROSOLS, ETC.)

Sometimes called 'glue sniffing' or volatile substance abuse (VSA).

What are they?

There is a wide range of solvents and volatile substances such as aerosols and gases often based on domestic and industrial products including solvent-based glues, lighter fuels such as butane gas, aerosols, typewriter correcting fluids, nail varnish remover, petrol, dry cleaning fluids, etc.

Medical use

None. These substances are in widespread domestic and industrial use.

How taken

The vapours given off by these substances are breathed in through the nose and/or mouth. In some cases the substance may be placed in a bag or put on a rag and then sniffed. In other cases it will be directly inhaled, e.g. aerosols squirted straight down the throat.

Extent of use

These substances are available in just about every household and many shops and workplaces. Some local surveys have found up to 20 per cent of 16-year-olds claiming to have used solvents at least once but long-term, regular use is relatively rare. There are often outbreaks of sniffing in local areas often for a short time. It is much more popular in summer than in winter, usually as an outdoor activity.

Effects

The effects are fast but short-lived – usually less than three quarters of an hour without a repeat dose. Breathing and heart rate slow. The effect is to feel light-headed and often dizzy. Some users feel dreamy and happy, but others say they feel sick and drowsy. Some users claim to see or hear things that are not there. As it wears off users feel drowsy and may experience a hangover.

Risks

Accidents are more likely as users can become unsteady and disorientated. Solvent use can lead to loss of consciousness. In most cases users quickly come round but there have been deaths from users choking on their own vomit. There is a serious risk of suffocation if the substance is used by putting it in a large bag that is then put over the head.

When squirted straight down the throat, aerosols and gases have resulted in instant deaths through heart failure or freezing of the airways. Between 60 and 150 young people have died each year using solvents in recent times but figures have declined in the 1990s.

Long-term exposure to some solvents in industrial settings has been shown to damage the brain, kidney and liver but it is not known how prolonged sniffing will affect these organs. In practice most risks seem to be acute, i.e. short term.

Tolerance can develop such that more is needed to get the same effect. Physical dependence is not a problem but psychological dependence can develop in some cases.

Reducing harm

If someone is determined to use solvents they could:

1. Never use solvents on their own.
2. Learn first aid to help others if needed.
3. Keep one person sober to mind the others.
4. If using a 'glue bag', use a small one and not place it over the head.
5. Avoid squirting aerosols or butane straight down the throat (squirting into a bag, on to a rag or up the sleeve of a coat or jumper before inhaling the fumes is less dangerous. This means the solvent is not as concentrated or – in the case of aerosols – as freezing cold).
6. Avoid use in dangerous environments where accidents are more likely (train tracks, roads, canal or river banks, derelict buildings, near busy roads, etc.).

STEROIDS

What are they?

Anabolic steroids are drugs that are similar to hormones, which are in the human body as growth and development agents. They can be made from natural and synthetic sources.

Other names

Common trade names include Dianabol, Durabolin, Nadrolone, and Stanozolol.

Medical use

Anabolic steroids are used to treat anaemia, thrombosis and breast cancer and for protein build-up after long periods of inactivity.

How taken

They are usually swallowed as pills or injected. They are often taken in cycles of a few weeks using then a few weeks off.

Extent of use

It is unclear how widespread their use is. In addition to their medical use they are available through some gyms, health clubs, sports clubs, etc. There have been reports that some young people have used steroids to improve their appearance as well as to increase strength and athletic performance.

Effects

These drugs build up body weight and increase the size of muscles. They also can make users feel more aggressive and better able to perform strenuous physical activity.

Risks

Heavy use can lead to physical harm such as liver abnormalities, water retention, high blood pressure, fertility problems in men, development of 'male' characteristics in females and growth problems in young users. Psychological dependence appears to be quite common. Users come to feel that they cannot perform well without steroids. Prolonged use of anabolic steroids can make users feel more aggressive and violent. If injected, there is the risk of blood-borne infections such as HIV and hepatitis if injecting equipment is shared. Injecting may also make it difficult to control the amount taken, so there is a risk of taking too much.

Reducing harm

If someone is determined to use steroids they could:

1. Be careful about the quantities used. Many users will not know much about this and need to find out.
2. Only use for short periods in strictly controlled ways.
3. Be aware of the risks of psychological dependence.
4. Be aware of the possible side effects and seek medical advice if needed.
5. Take particular care if injecting by carefully managing quantities taken and avoiding the risks of infection by not sharing needles.

TOBACCO

What is it?

Tobacco is the product of tobacco plants mainly grown in Third

World countries. The active drug is nicotine. Tobacco is made into cigarettes, cigars, pipe tobacco and snuff.

Street names
Backy, fags, snout.

Medical use
None.

How taken
Tobacco is usually smoked but can also be snorted up the nose as snuff or chewed in the mouth.

Extent of use
About one third of British adults smoke cigarettes. The numbers have been falling, especially among males. The number of teenagers smoking has grown recently, with young females outnumbering young male smokers.

Effects
The effects are very quick and one dose can last up to 30 minutes. Pulse rate and blood pressure increases. Regular users often say smoking a cigarette alleviates anxiety and stress, helps them concentrate and combats boredom. Some smokers also find it suppresses the appetite for food.

Risks
Tolerance develops quickly so more is needed to get the same effect. Most users become dependent and feel restless, irritable and depressed if they stop. Regular, long-term users have much greater risk of lung and some other cancers, heart disease, circulatory problems, bronchitis and ulcers. In the UK over 110,000 people die each year from the effects of smoking.

There is also a risk of health damage to other people who are nearby and may inhale the fumes. This 'passive' use of the drug has been claimed to cause several hundred deaths each year.

Reducing harm
If someone is determined to use tobacco they could try some of the following strategies:

1. Set a daily limit for numbers of cigarettes smoked.
2. Have a regular cigarette free day each week.
3. Limit where they smoke to certain places only – e.g. not at home, work or in the car.
4. Avoid smoking in front of children.
5. Avoid smoking in front of non-smokers and in places with poor ventilation.
6. Use low tar/extra filter brands where possible.
7. Only smoke half of any cigarette.
8. Avoid people who smoke and places where people smoke.
9. Use substitutes for cigarettes, including nicotine in other forms such as chewing gum and patches.
10. Switch to a pipe or cigars and not inhale the smoke.

TRANQUILLISERS

What are they?

These are synthetic drugs manufactured for medical use in the treatment of anxiety, depression, sleeplessness and epilepsy. They include minor tranquillisers such as Diazepam (Valium), Lorazepam (Ativan) and Chlorodiazepoxide (Librium) and sleeping tablets such as Nitrazepam (Mogadon), Flurazepam (Dalmane) and Euphynos (Temazepam). These drugs are collectively known as benzodiazepines.

Street names

Benzos, tranx. Mogadon are often called 'moggies'. Temazepam are called 'green or yellow eggs', 'jellies' and 'jelly babies', 'rugby balls' or 'temazzies'.

Medical use

Minor tranquillisers are mainly prescribed to relieve anxiety and some types are used as sleeping pills.

How taken

They are usually taken as medicines, swallowed as pills or capsules. They are also used in the same way on the street but some forms (especially temazepam) can be prepared for injection.

Extent of use

These are the most commonly prescribed drugs in the UK. There are over 20 million prescriptions for tranquillisers each year, 14 per cent of adults use them at some time in each year and 2.5 per cent use them regularly throughout the year. Twice as many females as males are prescribed these drugs. The full extent of street use is unclear, but it has greatly increased in recent years. Whilst some young people take them orally one particular type, Temazepam, is now commonly prepared for injection by heroin users.

Effects

These are sedative drugs. They slow down the operation of the central nervous system. They can make users drowsy and lethargic and possibly forgetful. They can relieve tension and anxiety and promote relaxation and calm. The effects begin after 10–15 minutes and can last up to six hours without repeating the dose.

Risks

Slowing down reactions and causing drowsiness can increase the risk of accidents whilst under the influence. Tolerance develops quickly, so more is needed to get the same effect. Dependence can develop quickly with regular use. Withdrawal from the drug can lead to anxiety, headaches and nausea. After high doses sudden withdrawal can be dangerous and result in fits.

After a relatively short time these drugs can be ineffective in producing their desired effects. As tolerance to the drug develops there is the risk of increasing dependence by taking more and more of the drugs. These higher doses can lead to confusion, anxiety and forgetfulness.

Although it is not possible to overdose fatally on a benzodiazepine on its own, they are much more dangerous in combination with other drugs, particularly alcohol. They have been implicated in a number of fatal overdoses when mixed in this way.

If tranquillisers are injected there can be serious damage to the veins and other blood vessels, particularly because the tablets and capsules are not designed for injection.

Reducing harm

If someone is determined to use tranquillisers they could try some of the following:

1. Not use with other drugs, especially alcohol or other sedatives.
2. Not drive or operate machinery whilst under the influence.
3. Not withdraw suddenly if dependent. Seek medical help and a gradual withdrawal programme.
4. If injecting, take care with quantities and avoid sharing injecting equipment.

OTHER DRUGS (GHB, KETAMINE, KHAT AND 'OVER-THE-COUNTER' MEDICINES)

GHB

GHB is gamma-hydroxybutyrate. It is also sometimes called GBH or 'liquid ecstasy'. It is a colourless, odourless liquid with a salty taste that is sold in small bottles and drunk. It is not illegal to be in possession of it and a bottle usually costs between £10 and £15. GHB is a sedative drug and, like alcohol, in small doses reduces inhibitions and may increase sexual interest. As more is taken the euphoric effects give way to the sedative effect. High doses have led to nausea, vomiting, muscle stiffness and disorientation. Very high doses have led to convulsions and coma. Although some people have been rushed to hospital after using GHB most tend to make a quick and full recovery. There have recently been a few deaths associated with consumption of large doses of GHB. It can be particularly dangerous if mixed with other drugs, including alcohol. Regular, long-term use may lead to dependence but not a lot is known of the effects of long-term use.

Ketamine

This drug found its way into the club and rave scene in major cities in 1992. It is a powder that is sniffed or a tablet. Street names include K, special K and super K. Ketamine has pain-killing effects and alters perception. Users report feelings of detachment and remoteness. At first it can give a rush of energy and a hallucinogenic effect, a bit like LSD. Little is known yet about the risks but it seems that tolerance and physical dependence are not a problem with ketamine.

Taking ketamine when feeling anxious or depressed could result in disturbing experiences. The pain-killing effect could also increase the risk of accidents. It is known that a large single dose can produce numbness and irregular muscle co-ordination. The risks of regular long-term use are not yet known. One additional risk is that of not knowing that you are taking ketamine. It came on to the UK drug scene by being sold as ecstasy. Quite a lot of ketamine is still being sold as ecstasy, although it is also now sold in its own right as well and in turn other drugs are now being sold as ketamine.

Khat

Khat is a green leafy plant that is widely grown in East Africa and the Arabian Peninsula. It has been chewed or prepared as a drink in some countries for centuries, being used in any everyday way – much as tea and coffee are widely used in the UK. Khat use is also known in the UK within some Ethiopian, Somalian and Yemeni communities and is regularly imported. Its active ingredients start to deteriorate a few days after harvesting, which means that it must be consumed fresh. UK law does not control the khat plant (although the active ingredients are controlled drugs). It is openly sold in some greengrocers. It is a stimulant drug and users often report initial mild euphoria and talkativeness followed by a feeling of calm. Chewing khat regularly may lead to mouth infections and there has been suggestion of it leading to oral cancer. Excessive use can lead to heart problems and loss of sex drive in men as well as trigger mental health problems such as anxiety, paranoia and depression. Whilst moderate, controlled use may not lead to many problems some commentators have been concerned about excessive use in some ethnic minority communities in the UK as a response to the experience of poverty and racism.

Over-the-counter (OTC) medicines

There are a number of medicines (cold remedies, cough syrups, travel sickness pills etc.) which are available without a prescription from chemists and which can be used to get a 'high'. Some of these drugs have stimulant or sedative effects. Examples are 'Gee's Linctus', 'Benylin' cough mixture, 'Night Nurse' or 'Codis' tablets many of which contain codeine or other similar drugs. Other OTC drugs have stimulant effects. Examples are 'Sudafed', 'Phenergan' or 'Do-Do' tablets. Some OTC medicines contain a mixture of stimulant and sedative drugs. One example is 'Day Nurse'.

Regular illegal drug users will sometimes resort to the use of OTC medicines if they cannot get their normal drug of choice. For example, heroin users might use some of the opioid-containing OTC medicines. Younger people might experiment with OTC medicines (or herbal remedies) to see if they can get a high. Rumours fly. 'Try some X and you'll get a buzz.' Sometimes the buzz comes and sometimes it does not. Some young people are ever optimistic and often reckless in their search for a new drug experience.

Appendix II
WHERE TO FIND OUT MORE

Helping organisations

In your locality

If you cannot find out which drug organisations and services exist in your local area, ring the National Drugs Helpline free on 0800 77 66 00. They should have details of all the drug services in your area.

You can also ring SCODA (Standing Conference on Drug Abuse) (Tel. 0171 928 9500), the national organisation for drug services in the UK.

National organisations

ADFAM
Waterbridge House, 32–36 Loman Street, London SE1 0EE. Tel. 0171 928 8900.
This is the national charity for the families and friends of drug users. It runs a national helpline and provides training courses, including courses for parents.

Alcohol Concern
Waterbridge House, 32–36 Loman Street, London SE1 0EE. Tel. 0171 928 7377. E-mail: alccon@popmail.dircon.co.uk
This is the national organisation for the UK's alcohol services and may provide information about alcohol and alcohol services.

Families Anonymous
The Doddington and Rollo Community Association, Charlotte Despard Avenue, Battersea, London SW11 5JE. Tel. 0171 498 4680
This is an organisation of local support groups for parents and friends of drug users in different parts of the country. It operates on a similar model to Alcoholics and Narcotics Anonymous.

The Health Education Authority
Trevelyan House, 30 Great Peter Street, London SW1P 2HW. Tel. 0171 222 5300. E-mail: hpic.enquiry@hea.org.uk
This is the national body that has the responsibility for leading health education in the UK. It runs information and education

campaigns often in conjunction with other organisations. One of its key areas is that of national drug education campaigns.

Healthwise

1st Floor, Cavern Court, 8 Mathew Street, Liverpool L2 6RE. Tel. 0151 227 4150. E-mail: info@healthwise.org.uk
This is a publisher of drug education books, manuals, games and computer programs used in schools, youth clubs and with parents and young people. It also has a school support unit which runs the UK's biggest regional drug education training programme for schools. Both the authors of this book work for Healthwise.

ISDD (Institute for the Study of Drug Dependence)

Waterbridge House, 32–36 Loman Street, London SE1 0EE. Tel. 0171 928 9500. E-mail: services@isdd.co.uk
This is the UK's main specialist library on drugs and drug use. It is a main source of up-to-date information on drugs in the UK. It produces a range of pamphlets on drugs and the bimonthly *Druglink* magazine.

Narcotics Anonymous

UK Service Office, 202 City Road, London EC1V 2PH. Tel. 0171 251 4007.
This is the co-ordinating office of a network of self-help groups for drug users based on Alcoholics Anonymous model. They also have a national helpline on 0171 730 0009.

National Drugs Helpline Tel. 0800 77 66 00

E-mail: network@netscot.co.uk
As the name suggests this is a free, confidential telephone advice line run 24 hours a day. It also can supply free copies of leaflets for young people and parents.

Release

388 Old Street, London EC1V 9LT. Tel. 0171 729 9904
24-hour helpline (0171 603 8654) for emergencies.
This is a national organisation concerned with legal rights. It has a particular interest in drugs and the law. It offers information and advice about legal and social aspects of drugs. Release also has a 'Drugs in Schools Helpline' offering confidential advice to young people and parents who are involved in drug incidents (Tel. 0345 36 66 66 during office hours).

SCODA (Standing Conference on Drug Abuse)
Waterbridge House, 32–36 Loman Street, London SE1 0EE. Tel.
0171 928 9500. E-mail: info@scoda.demon.co.uk
This is the national organisation of UK drug services. It publishes
information about drug services and works to increase the range
and quality of drug services in the UK.

Books and pamphlets to read

*Coping with a Nightmare – Family Feelings about Long Term
Drug Abuse*, ISDD 1994.
Based on interviews with families and parents about how they
have reacted to long-term, heavy drug use by their youngsters.

The D Word, ISDD 1998
Magazine for parents covering basic information and advice about
drugs. ISDD also produce two other drug magazines, *D Mag* for
aged 16 plus and *D Brief* for 11–14-year-olds.

Forbidden Drugs, P. Robson, Oxford University Press 1994.
Good paperback about different drugs, their use and drug policy.

Living with Drugs, M. Gossop, Ashgate 1993.
Excellent paperback covering social and historical aspects.

Street Drugs, A. Tyler, Hodder and Stoughton 1995.
Very readable paperback crammed full of information.

The User, A. Macfarlane, Oxford University Press 1996.
Paperback about young people's drug use that includes many
quotes from users and parents.

Computers and the Internet

There are a few computer programs and games which have
information about drugs. One of which, *DrugData 2*, is listed
below. You will also find that encyclopaedias like Encarta and
Hutchinson's have information about legal and illegal drugs.

You can also use the Internet to get information about drugs.
You can use a search facility to type in the word 'drugs' or anything more specific you want to find out more about. This will
link you to a vast range of websites. There are also many 'news-
groups' on the Internet where people correspond about drug

issues. But do take care. Some sites are useful and have accurate information. Others are much less useful. The 'anything goes' nature of the Internet means that many discussion groups are dominated by people who have very strong pro- or anti-drug views which are often based on little more than personal prejudices. Whilst they can be entertaining to view they may not contain much useful information. A few of the more informative websites are listed below.

Institute for the Study of Drug Dependence (ISDD) – the main UK source of accurate and up-to-date drug information.
http://www.isdd.co.uk

Alcohol concern
http://www.alcoholconcern.org.uk

Hyperreal Drugs Archive – a vast amount of information with links to many other sites.
http://www.hyperreal.com/drugs/

UK Cannabis Information Site
http://www.foobar.co.uk/users/ukcia/index.html

Some drug education resources for parents

(All can be obtained from Healthwise. Tel. 0151 227 4415)

The three resources listed below have been written by the authors of this book to help parents and young people to learn about drugs together at home.

The Drug Facts Card Game
This is a simple card game that will test your knowledge and provoke a great deal of discussion about drugs with your youngsters. The information is up-to-date and the cards include full colour pictures of drugs.

DrugData2
This is a computer program on CD-ROM with information about all aspects of drug use. It has been designed to run on any standard PC with a CD-ROM and includes sections on where drugs come from, what they look like, how they work within the body, what helping services there are in the UK and how to contact them. There are also sections on drugs and the law and

the paraphernalia used with drugs. The CD makes use of video footage to show how drugs are prepared for use. There is a parental control button to ensure that the CD is used responsibly.

What drugs look like
As the title suggests this is a video that shows all the main drug types and what they look like in use. There are sections on the paraphernalia used with drugs. The content of this video is also found in the CD-ROM *DrugData2* – listed above.

Drug Education Resources used in schools

The drug education and training packs listed below have been written or contributed to by the authors of this book and are designed to be used with groups of young people in schools or youth and community settings.

Taking Drugs Seriously 3
This is a comprehensive drug education package written by the authors of this book together with another colleague and covering facts, risk taking, attitudes, reducing harm, the law, giving and receiving help, etc. It is designed for young people aged 12 years upwards and includes a workshop for parents and governors.

Simply Drugs
This is a 'low literacy' drug education package for young people aged 11 years plus. It gives lots of ideas to educators on how they can educate young people about drugs without too much reading or writing on their part.

The Primary School Drugs Pack
This is a comprehensive drug education package for primary school ages. It covers policy and incident management issues as well as drug education in the primary school curriculum. It includes pupil activities and parent workshop materials.

Index